BAPTISTWAYPRESS®

Adult Bible Study Guide

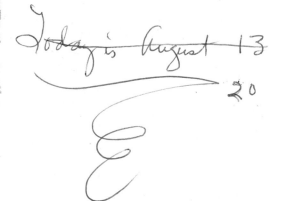

1 and 2 Timothy, Titus, Philemon

Howard Batson
Todd Still
Robert Shippey

BAPTISTWAYPRESS®

Dallas, Texas

For information, contact BAPTISTWAY PRESS, Baptist General Convention
of Texas, 333 North Washington, Dallas, TX 75246–1798.

BAPTISTWAY PRESS® is registered in U.S. Patent and Trademark Office.

Scripture marked NASB is taken from the New American Standard Bible®,
Copyright © The Lockman Foundation 1960, 1962, 1963, 1968, 1971, 1972,
1973, 1975, 1977, 1995. Used by permission. Unless otherwise indicated, all
Scripture quotations in the *Study Guide* materials on 1 Timothy are from the
New American Standard Bible®.

Scripture marked NRSV is taken from the New Revised Standard Version Bible,
copyright 1989, Division of Christian Education of the National Council of
the Churches of Christ in the United States of America. Used by permission.
All rights reserved. Unless otherwise indicated, all Scripture quotations in the
Study Guide materials on 2 Timothy, Titus, and Philemon are from the New
Revised Standard Version.

Scripture marked NIV is taken from The Holy Bible, New International Version
(North American Edition), copyright © 1973, 1978, 1984 by the International
Bible Society. Used by permission of Zondervan Publishing House.

BAPTISTWAY PRESS® Management Team
Executive Director, Baptist General Convention of Texas: Charles Wade
Director, Missions, Evangelism, and Ministry Team: Wayne Shuffield
Director, Bible Study/Discipleship Center: Dennis Parrott

Editor & publishing consultant: Ross West, Positive Difference Communications
Cover and Interior Design and Production: Desktop Miracles, Inc.
Cover Photo: Ancient Ephesus, www.bibleplaces.com

First edition: June 2006
ISBN: 1–931060–77–0

How to Make the Best Use of This Issue

Whether you're the teacher or a student—

1. Start early in the week before your class meets.

2. Overview the study. Review the table of contents and read the study introduction. Try to see how each lesson relates to the overall study.

3. Use your Bible to read and consider prayerfully the Scripture passages for the lesson. (You'll see that each writer has chosen a favorite translation for the lessons in this issue. You're free to use the Bible translation you prefer and compare it with the translation chosen for that unit, of course.)

4. After reading all the Scripture passages in your Bible, then read the writer's comments. The comments are intended to be an aid to your study of the Bible.

5. Read the small articles—"sidebars"—in each lesson. They are intended to provide additional, enrichment information and inspiration and to encourage thought and application.

6. Try to answer for yourself the questions included in each lesson. They're intended to encourage further thought and application, and they can also be used in the class session itself.

If you're the teacher—

A. Do all of the things just mentioned, of course. In the first session of the study, briefly overview the study by identifying with your class the date on which each lesson will be studied. Lead your class to write the date in the table of contents on page 7 and on the first page of each lesson. You might also find it helpful to make and post a chart that indicates the date on which each lesson will be studied. If all of your class has e-mail, send them an e-mail with the dates the lessons will be studied. (At least one church that uses BAPTISTWAY® materials for its classes places a sticker on the table of contents to identify the dates.)

B. Get a copy of the *Teaching Guide*, a companion piece to this *Study Guide*. The *Teaching Guide* contains additional Bible comments plus two teaching plans. The teaching plans in the *Teaching Guide* are intended to provide practical, easy-to-use teaching suggestions that will work in your class.

C. After you've studied the Bible passage, the lesson comments, and other material, use the teaching suggestions in the *Teaching Guide* to help you develop your plan for leading your class in studying each lesson.

D. You may want to get the additional adult Bible study comments—*Adult Online Bible Commentary*—by Dr. Jim Denison, pastor of

Park Cities Baptist Church, Dallas, Texas, that are available at www.baptistwaypress.org and can be downloaded free. An additional teaching plan plus teaching resource items are also available at www.baptistwaypress.org.

E. You also may want to get the enrichment teaching help that is provided on the internet by the *Baptist Standard* at www.baptiststandard.com. (Other class participants may find this information helpful, too.) Call 214–630–4571 to begin your subscription to the printed edition of the *Baptist Standard.*

F. Enjoy leading your class in discovering the meaning of the Scripture passages and in applying these passages to their lives.

1 and 2 Timothy, Titus, Philemon

7

august 20
aug 20

Introducing

1 TIMOTHY: Care for the Church

The name "pastoral letters" has been applied to 1 and 2 Timothy and Titus since the eighteenth century. The name indicates that these letters are about providing care in a pastoral manner to the church. They deal with "church care," with what we sometimes call "church administration," if by that we mean the broad range of care for the church's welfare.

First Timothy, the longest of these "pastoral letters," contains motivation, guidance, and encouragement for caring for the church. A special emphasis in this letter is on dealing with the challenge of "different doctrine" (1 Timothy 1:3, NRSV). Misplaced doctrinal emphases and blatantly false teachings threatened the early church's ministry, included the church at Ephesus, where Timothy served (1 Tim. 1:3).

The letter is identified as being from Paul to Timothy (1:1–2). It is written as a set of instructions for Timothy to know how to help the church in the challenges it faced. Timothy was younger and less experienced in guiding churches than was Paul.

Some of these instructions are among the more difficult to interpret and apply to our day in all of

Scripture. A prime example is the instructions in 1 Timothy 2:8–15 about women. In addition, as we Christians participate in our materialistic culture and demonstrate in many ways how much we value money, the instructions and warnings about money may be just as difficult to interpret and apply. Even so, the affirmation that "all Scripture is inspired by God" (2 Timothy 3:16)[1] calls us not to shy away from such passages but to seek faithfully their meaning and discover and apply as best we can the implications for our day.

Since 1 Timothy along with 2 Timothy, Titus, and Philemon in this study are all addressed to individuals, all can be considered "personal" to one degree or another, but they are not "private," applying only to that individual. They all speak in varying degrees to situations in the larger community of faith in the first century. Plus, as we will see as we study these letters, they *still* speak. We, though, need to make the effort to hear and understand in our own time and place.

The six lessons in this study of 1 Timothy will provide guidance in understanding and applying this brief but significant letter. The passages studied move sequentially through the letter and deal with almost all of it. One exception is 1 Timothy 5. To avoid repetition, the subject matter of that chapter is considered in a lesson from the Letter to Titus that deals with a similar subject (see lesson 11 on Titus 2:1–14).

1 TIMOTHY: CARE FOR THE CHURCH

Additional Resources for Studying 1 Timothy[2]

James D. G. Dunn. "The First and Second Letters to Timothy and the Letter to Titus." *The New Interpreter's Bible*. Volume XI. Nashville, Tennessee: Abingdon Press, 2000.

Gordon D. Fee. *1 and 2 Timothy*. New International Biblical Commentary. Peabody, Massachusetts: Hendrickson Publishers, 1988.

Donald Guthrie. *The Pastoral Epistles*. Revised edition. Tyndale New Testament Commentaries. Grand Rapids, Michigan: William B. Eerdmans Publishing Company, 1990.

E. Glenn Hinson. "1—2 Timothy and Titus." *The Broadman Bible Commentary*. Volume 11. Nashville, Tennessee: Broadman Press, 1971.

George W. Knight III. *Commentary on the Pastoral Epistles*. New International Greek Testament Commentary. Grand Rapids, Michigan: William B. Eerdmans Publishing Company, 1992.

Thomas D. Lea and Hayne P. Griffin, Jr. *1, 2 Timothy, Titus.* The New American Commentary. Volume 34. Nashville, Tennessee: Broadman Press, 1992.

A. T. Robertson. *Word Pictures in the New Testament.* Volume IV. Nashville, Tennessee: Broadman Press, 1931.

NOTES

1. Unless otherwise indicated, all Scripture quotations in this introduction and the lessons on 1 Timothy are from the New American Standard Bible (1995 edition).
2. Listing a book does not imply full agreement by the writers or BAPTISTWAY PRESS® with all of its comments.

Main Idea

Healthful Christian teaching and a life in accord with the gospel are based on one's recognition of God's mercy and grace.

Question to Explore

What's most important to you—God's mercy in your life or arguments about the details of religion?

LESSON ONE

Called to Healthful Teaching and Right Living

Study Aim

To explain how one's need for God's mercy and grace is the basis for healthful doctrine and right living

Study and Action Emphases

- Affirm the Bible as our authoritative guide for life and ministry
- Share the gospel with all people
- Develop a growing, vibrant faith
- Equip people for servant leadership

Quick Read

Paul called on Timothy to stop the false teachers in Ephesus from spreading their doctrines. Paul wanted Christians to focus on the gospel of Christ Jesus, which leads to love from a pure heart, a good conscience, and a sincere faith, and not to dabble in foolish teaching, which could lead only to ungodly living.

When I was in seminary, I discovered a television preacher who seemed most unusual. He sat on a stage and smoked a cigar, promising that he would give a prophetic secret just as soon as a set amount of money was raised. His band played music to drum up business while he used profanity to goad the television audience to call in their commitments so that he would have enough money to reveal the prophetic secret.

This wild, cigar-smoking preacher appeared to have much in common with Paul's opponents in Ephesus. They, too, had little regard for godly living and were peddling endless mysteries and secrets in order to make money. They were prophets for profit. Paul, in the midst of this chaos, called Timothy to lead the church back to sound biblical doctrine.

First Timothy is part of a collection known as the pastoral epistles (2 Timothy and Titus are also included in this collection). The pastoral epistles contain instructions about the administrative responsibilities of Timothy and Titus in the churches.

The pastoral epistles confront a brand of false teaching found in the early church. As Paul challenged this perverted version of Christianity, he called for sound doctrine that avoided the Jewish myths and disputes concerning the law that had become centerpieces of the false teachers' assertions.

1 Timothy 1:1–19a

1Paul, an apostle of Christ Jesus according to the commandment of God our Savior, and of Christ Jesus, who is our hope,

2to Timothy, my true child in the faith: Grace, mercy and peace from God the Father and Christ Jesus our Lord.

3As I urged you upon my departure for Macedonia, remain on at Ephesus so that you may instruct certain men not to teach strange doctrines, **4**nor to pay attention to myths and endless genealogies, which give rise to mere speculation rather than furthering the administration of God which is by faith. **5**But the goal of our instruction is love from a pure heart and a good conscience and a sincere faith. **6**For some men, straying from these things, have turned aside to fruitless discussion, **7**wanting to be teachers of the Law, even though they do not understand either what they are saying or the matters about which they make confident assertions.

8But we know that the Law is good, if one uses it lawfully, **9**realizing the fact that law is not made for a righteous person, but for those who are lawless and rebellious, for the ungodly and sinners, for the unholy and profane, for those who kill their fathers or mothers, for murderers **10**and immoral men and homosexuals and kidnappers and liars and perjurers, and whatever else is contrary to sound teaching, **11**according to the glorious gospel of the blessed God, with which I have been entrusted.

12I thank Christ Jesus our Lord, who has strengthened me, because He considered me faithful, putting me into service, **13**even though I was formerly a blasphemer and a persecutor and a violent aggressor. Yet I was shown mercy because I acted ignorantly in unbelief; **14**and the grace of our Lord was more than abundant, with the faith and love which are found in Christ Jesus. **15**It is a trustworthy statement, deserving full acceptance, that Christ Jesus came into the world to save sinners, among whom I am foremost of all. **16**Yet for this reason I found mercy, so that in me as the foremost, Jesus Christ might demonstrate His perfect patience as an example for those who would believe in Him for eternal life. **17**Now to the King eternal, immortal, invisible, the only God, be honor and glory forever and ever. Amen.

18This command I entrust to you, Timothy, my son, in accordance with the prophecies previously made concerning you, that by them you fight the good fight, **19**keeping faith and a good conscience. . . .

Spurn Speculation (1:1–4)

Our rules for writing letters call for us to wait to identify the sender until the final words of a letter (Sincerely yours, John). Paul's letters, though, followed a different format, as follows: sender (Paul), recipient (Timothy), greeting (grace, mercy, and peace), and often (although not in this case) a word of thanks or praise. While 1 Timothy was written to an individual,

Paul was also communicating to the Ephesian church through Timothy. At the letter's conclusion, Paul wrote, "Grace be with you" (6:21; "you" is plural). Knowing that some Ephesian believers were turning away from the gospel of grace, Paul asserted his authority by declaring that his apostleship found its origin in God's (and Christ's) command on the Damascus Road (Acts 9:15; 22:14–15; 26:14–18).

Paul's gospel is a gospel of grace (1 Tim. 1:2, 14). "Grace" was Paul's one-word sermon for God's saving act in Christ, an act that made God's good favor available to undeserving sinners.

Crowds will gather for the spectacular, the mysterious, and the intriguing. Many preachers have learned well the tricks of filling the sanctuary. Topics of endless speculation and hot debate will often draw the throngs. Pretend to be peddling a secret, and everyone will gather to hear the glamorous revelation. Seminars advertising prophecy secrets or mysterious studies about angels will often pull in the people while less flamboyant topics like service and stewardship will leave the auditorium with a hollow ring from empty pews. People tend to be attracted to intriguing teachers who promise a new spin and a newly revealed truth.

While it is difficult to determine the content of the false teaching at Ephesus based on the admonitions against it, we can attempt to project what Paul's opponents were arguing. In presenting their "different teaching" (1:3, my translation), these opponents were advocating a skewed form of Judaism that overemphasized law and limited the role of God's grace.

These teachers loved endless debate about the minutia of the Old Testament law and quibbled constantly about words (see also 6:3–4; 20–21). Casting aside the gospel of grace as preached by Paul, these heretics were promoting speculative myths based on minor characters listed in Old Testament genealogies (see also 4:7).

They were prophets for profit.

Paul referred to their teaching as "worldly fables fit only for old women" (4:7; "old wives' tales," NRSV). The result was unacceptable behavior.

Seek Sound Teaching (1:5–11)

We all know how to lose weight. The formula is actually quite simple. We must burn more calories than we consume. We can increase the number of calories we burn by exercising and/or reduce our caloric intake by eating less food or eating less calorie-laden foods.

We all know that a reasonable diet of fruits, vegetables, and lean meats combined with a regular exercise program will lead us to the most healthful lifestyle. We are always, nonetheless, searching for new wisdom when it comes to parting with our pounds. There are diets to please everyone looking for that mysterious magic that will shed the pounds without demanding discipline in the diet. For example, have you heard of

"The Pasta-Chocolate Diet"? While you might have thought that you must stay away from these guilt goodies, the Pasta-Chocolate Diet actually steers you toward these two delightful delicacies.[1]

Or how about "The Incredible Ice Cream Diet"? Prevention.com claims new research shows that ice cream may actually melt away fat, helping you lose extra pounds faster than if you'd abstained![2]

If you're not into chocolate or ice cream, you might want to try "The Amazing Peanut Butter Diet." This is sure to satisfy your longing for that rich, sticky goo that you craved as a child.[3]

"The 7-Day-All-You-Can-Eat-Diet" is the diet I'm interested in! On Monday, you can consume all the fruit you want, except bananas. On Tuesday, you can have all the vegetables you want. On Wednesdays, you can eat all the fruits and vegetables you desire. This diet continues to allow you to have all you want, "all you can eat!"[4]

"Grace" was Paul's one-word sermon for God's saving act in Christ. . . .

If none of these work for you, don't fret. There are plenty of others to choose from: The Popcorn Diet, The Three-Day Diet, The Seven-Day Diet, or The Cabbage Soup Diet![5]

While we all know fad diets will not fade away our fat, we are not attracted by a solid and diversified diet that leads us to a balanced and healthful meal. On the contrary, we are drawn to mysterious meal plans that promise the unleashing of some great secret that will allow us to eat delicious foods, eat what we want, and still shed the pounds.

In the same way, the enemies of Paul were not interested in Paul's gospel of service and sacrifice centered on grace received from Christ Jesus. Rather, they were always searching and debating new mysteries that promised enlightenment. In chapter 6, Paul asserted that their "different doctrine" did not "agree with sound words" (6:3). For Paul, the sound words to be sought were the ethical teachings of Jesus, which—unlike his opponents' fruitless discussions—lead to a Christlike life (6:3).

Timothy was to stop the opponents of Paul and the gospel from spreading their speculative and spurious debates. He was to guide the church in healthful Christian teaching that yields godly living (1:5). Paul's goal was to lead Timothy to guide the church away from this false teaching and toward a spirit of love. This love comes from a heart cleansed from sin, a conscience free from guilt, and a faith formed in sincerity (1:5).

Pretend to be peddling a secret, and everyone will gather to hear the glamorous revelation.

The false teachers pretended to be experts on Jewish law (1:7), but they had, in reality, misunderstood the very role the law played in leading people to Christ (see also Galatians 3:24). Paul asserted that the law is for the ungodly (1:9). In Galatians 3:23—4:7 and Romans 7:7–25, Paul suggested that the law serves to expose the depth of our depravity. From Paul's examples in 1 Timothy 1:8–11, we can conclude that the false teachers were dabbling in the law of Moses, perhaps the Ten Commandments. The opponents were probably also saying that Paul had rejected the law. On the contrary, Paul affirmed the goodness of the law as long as it is used as God intended. The law does not apply to those who live under God's grace, which flows from the story of Jesus. For the follower of Christ ("righteous person," 1:9), godly living is a result of an inward transformation produced by the presence of God.

> *. . . Godly living is a result of an inward transformation produced by the presence of God.*

The ungodly are described by a vice list that parallels the Ten Commandments. The first three couplets ("lawless and rebellious," "ungodly and sinners," and "unholy and profane," 1:9) reflect the sins committed by Paul's opponents in Ephesus. The final offenses, offenses against people, remind the reader of the Ten Commandments, which address sins against humanity, as follows:

"those who kill their fathers or mothers"	"Honor your father and your mother" (Exodus 20:12; Deuteronomy 5:16).
"murderers"	"You shall not murder" (Exodus 20:13; Deuteronomy 5:17).
"immoral men," "homosexuals"	"You shall not commit adultery" (Exodus 20:14; Deuteronomy 5:18).
"kidnappers"	"You shall not steal" (Exodus 20:15; Deuteronomy 5:19).

"liars," "perjurers"	"You shall not bear false witness" (Exodus 20:16; Deuteronomy 5:20).[6]

Unlike their "strange doctrines" (1:3), the "sound teaching" (1:10) of Paul's "glorious gospel" (1:10) did not lead to ungodly behavior that breaks the law. "Sound teaching" is an often repeated theme in the pastoral epistles (see 6:3; 2 Timothy 1:13; 4:3; Titus 1:9, 13; 2:2, 8). Borrowing medical terms, Paul was referring to the healthiness of teaching found in the gospel as opposed to the "morbid craving" (6:4, NRSV) or "unhealthy interest" (NIV) of the false teachers whose "talk will spread like gangrene" (2 Tim. 2:17).[7]

> . . . The enemies of Paul were not interested in Paul's gospel of service and sacrifice centered on grace received from Christ Jesus.

Follow My Faith (1:12–19a)

In verse 11, Paul had spoken of "the glorious gospel" of God. Paul next applied that glorious gospel to his own life, giving his testimony. In this closing part of the chapter, Paul focused on God's grace as it is given in Christ. Unlike the law, grace brings the followers of Christ to faith and love and culminates in eternal life (1 Tim.1:14, 16).

Paul saw his conversion to Christianity as an act of God's grace (see also 1 Corinthians 15:9–10; Galatians 1:13–16). Paul, who had been a persecutor of

God's people, the church, was changed by the grace of God. In response to God's grace, Paul found faith (Romans 3:22–25; Ephesians 2:8).

If grace leads to faith, then faith leads to acts of love (Galatians 5:6). Faith and love are the result of a relationship with the Savior. The Ephesian opponents, on the other hand, turned away from faith and love (1 Tim. 1:5–6) and had, therefore, rejected this gospel of grace.

Note the words "It is a trustworthy statement" in 1:15. Paul used this expression four more times in the pastoral epistles (3:1; 4:9; 2 Tim. 2:11; Titus 3:8). The expression introduces statements that were currently being used in the churches and were acknowledged as "trustworthy." Stating that Christ came into the world to save sinners, Paul set forth a central Christian truth, indeed, a "trustworthy statement."

Paul's goal was to lead Timothy to guide the church away from this false teaching and toward a spirit of love.

Paul never strayed from the truth that salvation is for sinners. He was well aware of his own sinful nature, saying that he was "foremost" among sinners (1 Tim. 1:15). Understanding the depth of his sin allowed Paul to understand the magnitude of God's mercy (1:16). Paul called for the Ephesians to follow his example (1:16), thus living a life of faith in Christ. The word used for "example" is a word that could be translated as *a pattern*, like an outline sketch by an artist. Reflecting on the mercies of God, Paul was prompted to praise God with a doxology (1:17). Finally, he called on Timothy again (1:18) to "fight the good fight," thus embracing the gospel of grace he had received.

Kindred Spirit

Paul invested himself in Timothy's life. More than any other companion, Timothy accompanied Paul on his journeys, beginning sometime during Paul's second missionary journey (see Acts 16:1). Paul described Timothy as "my fellow worker" (Romans 16:21), as "God's fellow worker" (1 Thessalonians 3:2), as "my beloved and faithful child in the Lord" (1 Corinthians 4:17), as "genuinely . . . concerned for your welfare" (Philippians 2:19–20), and as a person of "proven worth" (Philippians 2:22). Paul ultimately called him his "brother" (2 Corinthians 1:1; Colossians 1:1) but also "my son" (1 Timothy 1:18). He declared, "I have no one else of kindred spirit" (Philippians 2:20). In the end, during Paul's projected second Roman imprisonment, he called for Timothy to come to his side (2 Tim. 4:9).

Timothy descended from a long line of faith—a faith that resided in his grandmother Lois (2 Tim. 1:5) and his mother Eunice, a Jewish-Christian woman (Acts 16:1). Timothy's father was a Gentile. We can suppose that Timothy became a Christian through the influence of his mother and the church leaders in Lystra who had heard the gospel through Paul and Silas.

Timothy had been helpful to Paul, but we also know that Paul was constantly encouraging Timothy, who was youthful (1 Tim. 4:12) and frequently ill (5:23).[8]

Survey of Sins

In more than one of his letters, Paul offered his readers a catalog of sins, called "vice lists" by scholars. Such lists are found in Romans 1:29–31; 1 Corinthians 5:11; 6:9–10; Galatians 5:19–21; and 2 Timothy 3:2–4. In each case, the list seems to be adapted to the context to which Paul wrote. For example, we detected in the list from 1 Timothy that the first three couplets relate to the lawless behavior of the false teachers. No single sin is specifically repeated in all the lists. Read the various sin lists and note their similarities and differences.

The Authorship of the Pastoral Epistles

According to the text of 1 and 2 Timothy and Titus, Paul was the author. More than any other books attributed to Paul in the New Testament, the authorship of the pastoral epistles is debated by scholars. The question about Paul's authorship stems from several factors, including a different vocabulary and writing style when compared with Paul's other letters.

I, however, fully attribute these letters to Paul. Ancient writers often used secretaries, called *amanuenses*, who had freedom in expressing the author's thoughts with words of their own choosing. Also in favor of Paul's authorship is the fact that the early tradition of the church strongly attributes these letters to Paul. In fact, only Romans and 1 Corinthians have stronger backing from the early church. While many claim that these letters were written in Paul's name by someone else, the early church did not accept writing in the name of another—writing pseudonymously. Paul himself warned against any such forgeries that might bear his name (2 Thess. 2:2; 3:17). Too, only Paul would describe himself as the "foremost" of sinners (1 Tim. 1:15).

Difficulties arise when we attempt to place the writing of the pastoral epistles within the life of Paul as presented in Acts. Paul, however, might have been released from his first Roman imprisonment, where the Book of Acts ends, and allowed a time of freedom. We could account for the events described in the pastoral epistles during that time. He might then have been imprisoned in Rome a second time.

Paul possibly wrote 1 Timothy and Titus between the imprisonments and 2 Timothy during his second imprisonment just before his death. Of course, given the uncertainty of these issues, we must always leave room for other opinions in regard to how these books fit within the life of the apostle.

Questions

1. What teachers or movements in our day parallel the false teachers found in Ephesus? In what ways?

2. Why do some Christians tend to follow new teachers, even people who are not grounded in a community of faith, a church?

3. What fruitless discussions are taking place in the church today?

4. Why would Paul call himself the "foremost" sinner?

5. What are the basic thoughts found in Paul's "sound teaching"?

6. In describing basic Christian teaching, what other words could follow Paul's introduction, "It is a trustworthy statement"?

NOTES

1. "The Pasta-Chocolate Diet," www.idiet4u.com/diets/pastachocolate.html
2. See "The Incredible Ice Cream Diet" at www.prevention.com.
3. See "Our Amazing Peanut Butter Diet" at www.prevention.com.
4. "7 Day All You Can Eat Diet," www.idiet4u.com/diets/7dayayce.html
5. "A Few Fad Diets," http://dietbites.com/article0159.html
6. William D. Mounce. *Pastoral Epistles*, Word Biblical Commentary (Nashville: Thomas Nelson Publishers, 2000), 30.
7. Gordon D. Fee, *1 and 2 Timothy, Titus*, New International Biblical Commentary (Peabody, MA: Hendrickson Publishers, 1988), 46.
8. G. F. Hawthorne, "Timothy," *The New International Standard Bible Encyclopedia*, vol. 4 (Grand Rapids: Eerdmans, 1988), 857–858.

Main Idea

Prayer for governmental leaders is aimed at creating a peaceful climate in which the gospel can be lived and shared most freely.

Question to Explore

Why pray for governmental leaders?

LESSON TWO

Pray for Freedom to Live Faithfully

Study Aim

To describe the relation of prayer for governmental leaders to living and sharing the gospel freely

Study and Action Emphases

- Affirm the Bible as our authoritative guide for life and ministry
- Share the gospel with all people
- Develop a growing, vibrant faith

Quick Read

Because God wants all people to be saved, Christ has given his life as a ransom for everyone. Thus, Paul urged the churches to pray for everyone, even pagan leaders. Demonstrating godly lives and good citizenship would create a political climate in which the gospel could spread.

When Reverend David Thomas stepped into the pulpit of the Broad Run Baptist Church in Virginia each Sunday, he might have to duck a punch or dodge a bullet. In the days before freedom of religion was guaranteed, representatives of the state church actually assaulted Pastor Thomas and disturbed his services. He was once even pulled down from the pulpit and dragged out the door in a barbarous manner. On another occasion, somebody tried to shoot him while he was preaching.

As Thomas grew older, he also grew tired of the pounding that often accompanied his preaching Baptist doctrine. He, therefore, recruited an assistant pastor, Amos Thompson, to fill the pulpit for him when the ruffians were going to be rowdy. Amos was a gigantic young man who was well known for his fabulous feats of strength.

On one occasion, the old pastor was warned that if he preached on Sunday he was going to be beaten black and blue. Because he knew they were coming to get him, he invited the young, vigorous Amos Thompson to preach in his place.

A great multitude assembled that Sunday. Some wanted to hear the preaching of the gospel while others wanted "ring side" pews. To their surprise, instead of declining David they found able Amos preaching powerfully. When the hecklers saw the brawny biceps on this young Baptist pastor, they decided they just might let him finish his sermon undisturbed!

Lesson 2: Pray for Freedom to Live Faithfully

During this early period in American history, Baptists were beaten, fined, imprisoned, and exiled from some colonies because they didn't agree with the officially sanctioned church.[1]

Political environments can influence greatly a religious community's ability to thrive. Historically, Baptists have sought religious freedom—not only for themselves but for others as well. Baptists have always wanted all people to answer only to God and not to governing authorities for their religious beliefs. Baptists were birthed in the battle for freedom to differ from the state church. Resisting forced conformity to the religious views of the state, Baptists have played a pivotal role in establishing the religious freedom enjoyed by Americans today. In his address made on May 16, 1920, on the steps of the United States Capitol, George Truett quoted John Locke's statement, "Baptists were the first propounders of absolute liberty, just and true liberty, equal and impartial liberty."[2]

The "wall of separation" was a metaphor popularized by Thomas Jefferson to describe the relationship between the church and the state. However, it was first coined by Roger Williams, a Baptist leader.[3] Like the Baptists in the American colonies, the Ephesians needed a political environment that would allow the good news of the kingdom of God to find firm root, unhindered by the governing powers.

1 Timothy 2:1–7

¹First of all, then, I urge that entreaties and prayers, petitions and thanksgivings, be made on behalf of all men, ²for kings and all who are in authority, so that we may lead a tranquil and quiet life in all godliness and dignity. ³This is good and acceptable in the sight of God our Savior, ⁴who desires all men to be saved and to come to the knowledge of the truth. ⁵For there is one God, and one mediator also between God and men, the man Christ Jesus, ⁶who gave Himself as a ransom for all, the testimony given at the proper time. ⁷For this I was appointed a preacher and an apostle (I am telling the truth, I am not lying) as a teacher of the Gentiles in faith and truth.

Prayers for All People (2:1–2)

Some scholars argue that chapters 2 and 3 are an independent manual of church organization. According to this view, these chapters have little to do with the Ephesian setting. A closer look, however, reveals that Paul, even if he was using well-known Christian traditions, was confronting his opponents' view. Paul's opponents proposed that God's salvation was available to only a limited few.

In the previous section, Paul had made clear that salvation is the fruit of God's mercy and grace, a grace that was given to Paul himself (1 Timothy 1:12–17).

Paul had already promoted a central Christian teaching by asserting that "Christ Jesus came into the world to save sinners" (1 Tim. 1:15). In chapter 2, Paul continued his emphasis on an inclusive salvation by declaring that God desires for all to be saved (2:4) and Christ Jesus gave himself as a ransom for all (2:6).

The prayers mentioned address Paul's larger focus on a salvation made available to everyone (2:1). Paul began his teaching on salvation by asking the Ephesians to utter prayers on behalf of all people (2:1). He so strongly advocated that salvation was available to anyone who might believe that he used the Greek word meaning "all" with reference to people four times in this brief section (2:1, 2, 4, 6). Because God wants all people to be saved, the Ephesian Christians were to pray for everyone, even pagan kings and those in authority.

Baptists were birthed in the battle for freedom to differ from the state church.

With his opening phrase, "First of all, then," Paul was connecting his plea for an inclusive view of salvation with his previous charge to Timothy to stop the false teachers from spreading their strange doctrines that apparently included a restricted view of salvation (1:1–4). Prayer for the salvation of all people is "first of all" in rank of priority for Paul.

Paul used four different words that can be translated *prayers*. The first of the four, "entreaties," is a common word for Paul. This word often describes a cry for help. In the presence of a pressing necessity, we entreat God. The second word, "prayers," is a more general term that occurs in some form more than 120 times in the New Testament. The third word, "petitions," is a more unusual word that is used only in here and in 1 Timothy 4:5, where it is translated "prayer." The word carries with it the idea of approaching God in boldness or confidence. The word probably represents prayers that are made on behalf of others, carrying the idea of interceding before God.

> Baptists have played a pivotal role in establishing the religious freedom enjoyed by Americans today.

The final word, "thanksgivings," was often used by Paul to express gratitude to God in the opening of his letters (Philippians 1:3; Colossians 1:3; 1 Thessalonians 1:2; 2 Thessalonians 1:3; Philemon 4). In our passage, it represents a prayer in which thanks is given.

While we want to appreciate the different nuances found in each of these four words for prayer, we should not overemphasize them individually. They combine together to form a harmonizing quartet that called for the Ephesian Christians to pray for the salvation of everyone.

When they prayed for "all" people, Paul wanted to make certain that the Ephesian Christians included kings and leaders. The false teachers were not only disrupting the church but also tarnishing the reputation of the church before pagan authorities. Christians, on the contrary, must live their lives in such a way that "the name of God . . . may not be spoken against" (1 Tim. 6:1). Paul made a similar argument in 1 Thessalonians 4:11–12. There he also promoted "leading a quiet life" (note the similar language to 1 Tim. 2:2) to "win the respect of outsiders" (1 Thess. 4:12, NIV). Paul's opponents were living the lives of "busybodies" (1 Tim. 5:13; compare 2 Thess. 3:11). By living in such a manner, they were pulling down the reputation of the church. When describing the Christian goal of leading a "tranquil and quiet life in all godliness and dignity," Paul was not calling the church to silence of speech, but rather to the tranquility that comes from a reverent life (2:2).

Good citizenship would allow the church to grow freely without hindrance or interruption from the state.

Paul desired for the church to win the respect of pagan authorities by displaying godly lifestyles (see Romans 13:1–5; Colossians 4:5–6; 1 Thess. 4:11–12; and 2 Thess. 3:12). Good citizenship would allow the church to grow freely without hindrance or interruption from the state. While Paul could not have hoped for full religious freedom in the Roman Empire, he was trying to create an atmosphere in which Christians could expand their numbers, unhindered by political powers.

Baptists have sought to follow this scriptural mandate to pray for governing authorities and live exemplary lives. We have not courted the endorsement of the state for our religious beliefs, however. The very center of our Baptist beginnings includes seeking the freedom to worship with neither the state's blessing nor the state's curse.[4]

Imagine for a moment that a business transfer moves your family to Utah—to Salt Lake City. Because there are few Baptists there, you will not have any political clout. Now that you find yourself surrounded by another religion that dominates the political scene, do you want the public school to deliver devotions to your children? Think carefully, because in Salt Lake City the teacher is most likely to be Mormon and the devotional book being used might well be the *Book of Mormon*.

Baptists have sought to follow this scriptural mandate to pray for governing authorities and live exemplary lives.

Baptists have always fervently declared that there is only one way to heaven, through God's Son Christ Jesus (John 14:6). Nonetheless, we have always been willing to defend another person's right to worship as the person so chooses even if he or she wants to worship a tree. Isaac Backus (1724–1806), one of the greatest spokespeople for religious liberty in America, argued that true religion is voluntary obedience to God.

When the United States Constitution first appeared in 1787, Baptists were shocked that the Constitution said nothing about religious liberty.[5] The Baptists, behind John Leland (1754–1841), worked diligently to amend the Constitution so that it provided religious liberty.[6] James Madison, backed by the Baptists, set forth the First Amendment, which reads,

"Congress shall make no law respecting an establishment of religion, or prohibiting the free exercise thereof. . . ."[7]

The Purpose of the Prayers (2:3–7)

Returning to his broader argument for an inclusive salvation, Paul proposed several reasons the Ephesian Christians should pray for everyone: (1) God is well pleased with prayer for the salvation of others because God wishes all people to be saved (1 Tim. 2:3–4); (2) salvation for everyone has been made available by the one Mediator, Jesus, who bridges the gap between God and humanity by giving himself as "a ransom for all" (2:6); and (3) including the Gentiles in the scope of salvation is the very ministry to which Paul had been called (2:7).

> *God desires for everyone to accept the truth of the gospel (2:4).*

God is not satisfied with only our salvation or that of an elitist few. God desires for everyone to accept the truth of the gospel (2:4). Calling God "our Savior" was a way to emphasize both that God is the originator of our salvation and that we are already in the process of receiving salvation (compare Philippians 1:28; 1 Thess. 5:9). The false teachers' truncated gospel promoted salvation for the few by employing foolish debates that appealed to humanity's insatiable desire for mysteries (see lesson one). Against this view,

Paul promoted God's good news, which was available to everyone. Paul emphasized that God himself desires that all people both hear and grasp his message of salvation.

Paul next asserted that there is but one God and one Mediator who gave himself as a ransom for all. In the midst of a polytheistic (many gods) culture, ancient Israel was always to declare that there was only one God. Israel was never, however, to argue that God was her God exclusively. To say "there is one God" is not only to say that there are no other gods, but also to say that this one God is for all people.[8] Jesus Christ is the one Mediator, the go-between for bringing God and sinful humanity together. As witnessed in the death of Christ, Paul asserted that now is "the proper time" for showing God's mercy to all (1 Tim. 2:6).

> Jesus Christ is the one Mediator, the go-between for bringing God and sinful humanity together.

Baptist churches have recently experienced the growth of a theology that resembles that of Paul's opponents in Ephesus. Like the Ephesian false teachers, some in Baptist circles have promoted the idea that Christ died for the few and not the many. These teachers have been teaching what is called a *limited atonement*. Salvation, according to this limited view, is available only for the chosen rather than for all who might place their faith in Christ Jesus. The view holds that God in his eternal plans and in his secret counsel has, according to this Ephesian-like teaching, chosen some of his fallen creatures for himself. The view further teaches that God never tells why some are chosen and some are not. Thus, as this view states, God, in his complete sovereignty, sends his Son to die only for the "elect" rather than for everyone.

The problem with this viewpoint, of course, is that it is in direct contradiction to Paul's clear teaching, here and elsewhere, that Christ has died for *all*. The New Testament is clear that Christ's death was designed to include all of humankind whether or not all eventually believed.

The New Testament is clear that Christ's death was designed to include all of humankind whether or not all eventually believed.

This passage, along with many others, teaches that Christ died for *all*. We must allow the word *all* to have its usual and full meaning. Many passages make little sense if we do not allow *all* to mean everyone (see Isaiah 53:6; 1 Tim. 2:1–6; 4:10; 1 John 2:2). Scripture makes clear that Christ is the Savior of the whole world (John 1:29; 3:16).

While several passages do assert that Christ died for "his people," these do not exclude the larger teaching that Christ also died for everyone (see Matthew 1:21; John 10:11; Acts 20:28; Ephesians 5:25). To say that Christ died for the church is not to exclude the fact that he also died for all of humanity.

Before Baptist churches begin to embrace any teaching that asserts that Christ did not die for everyone, they first should study carefully Paul's response to the troubling doctrine of the Ephesian teachers. Paul closed this section by demonstrating that his very ministry was shaped by God's inclusive plan of salvation. Paul himself was called to be a messenger to the Gentiles, the very people whom the opponents in Ephesus were excluding. Therefore, the Ephesians were to pray for the salvation of everyone.

"One Mediator"—"Ransom for All" (1 Timothy 2:5-6)

By using the term *mediator* to describe Jesus, Paul pictured Jesus as the negotiator between God and humanity. As our negotiator, Christ has established a new relationship between God and his people that did not previously exist. Paul's use of the Greek word translated "ransom" in 2:6 is the only New Testament occurrence of the word. Outside of New Testament writings, this word (and related words) describes the setting free of captives taken in war or the liberation of slaves from their master. The price paid for freedom was described as a "ransom." Paul was saying that Jesus' death is the price paid for our release from captivity to sin and death. Christ's death substituted for our death.

Prayers for People

If you were to be honest with yourself, could you list the names of five people for whom you have prayed in regard to their relationship with Christ? Praying for *all* people to have a saving relationship with God through Christ Jesus was a priority for Paul. Who should be on your prayer list? Who are you hoping will begin the pilgrimage of faith? A family member? A co-worker? Or perhaps a close friend? Who needs you to bring his or her name before God today? Pray for those who need Christ!

Questions

1. Why do Christians often fail to pray for people who need to discover salvation through Christ?

2. Why do you think Paul used the term "all" four times in this passage?

3. Why is it tempting to seek the government's endorsement for our own personal religious beliefs?

4. Why have Baptists grown from a persecuted minority in colonial America to the largest Protestant denomination in America?

NOTES

1. H. Leon McBeth, *The Baptist Heritage* (Nashville: Broadman Press, 1987), 270–271.
2. George W. Truett, "Baptists and Religious Liberty," *Christian Ethics Today* (February 2001), 22. See also www.bjconline.org/resources/pubs/pub_truett_address.htm.
3. McBeth, 254.
4. McBeth, 256–257.
5. McBeth, 280–282.
6. Bill J. Leonard, *Baptist Ways: A History* (Valley Forge: Judson Press, 2003), 130–132.
7. See www.archives.gov/national-archives-experience/charters/bill_of_rights_transcript.html.
8. Gordon D. Fee, *1 and 2 Timothy, Titus*, New International Biblical Commentary (Peabody, MA: Hendrickson Publishers, 1988), 65.

Focal Text

1 Timothy 2:8–15

Background

1 Timothy 2:8–15

Main Idea

Christian women and men are to conduct themselves in ways that show reverence for God.

Question to Explore

So what is a woman's place?

LESSON THREE

Women and Men in the Church

Study Aim

To identify implications for current church life of Paul's teachings about appropriate behavior for Christian women and men

Study and Action Emphases

- Affirm the Bible as our authoritative guide for life and ministry
- Develop a growing, vibrant faith
- Include all God's family in decision-making and service
- Value all people as created in the image of God
- Encourage healthy families
- Equip people for servant leadership

Quick Read

In this passage Paul addressed both men and women. He called on the men to avoid disputes during times of prayer. He admonished the women to dress modestly, be known for their good works, and avoid disrupting public worship.

She had a big decision to make. Having traveled more than 8,000 miles from Amarillo, Texas, to Uganda, Africa, to share the gospel, the pastor and his wife were devastated when he suddenly became ill during the mission trip and was unable to preach. Preaching the gospel had been the primary purpose of the trip to Uganda. Now, with his sickness, they had to sit in silence.

The pastor's wife had to decide. The Ugandans had suggested that she fill the pulpit because they hoped that the revival services could continue despite the preacher's illness. Back home, however, she would have never considered preaching from the pulpit a possibility. Would she disappoint the Ugandans who were eager to hear the word of God? Would she carry her American restrictions across the continents? Would she allow their trip to fizzle into little more than fruitless fanfare, or would she preach the messages in the place of her husband? What would her home church have to say when word of the woman preacher returned? What does the Bible say about a woman preaching or teaching?

All these questions swirled in the mind of the pastor's wife because she faced a decision—a decision that called for her to discern between timeless, scriptural truths and limited, cultural traditions. Would she stand and preach or sit silently?

1 Timothy 2:8–15

8Therefore I want the men in every place to pray, lifting up holy hands, without wrath and dissension.

9Likewise, I want women to adorn themselves with proper clothing, modestly and discreetly, not with braided hair and gold or pearls or costly garments, **10**but rather by means of good works, as is proper for women making a claim to godliness. **11**A woman must quietly receive instruction with entire submissiveness. **12**But I do not allow a woman to teach or exercise authority over a man, but to remain quiet. **13**For it was Adam who was first created, and then Eve. **14**And it was not Adam who was deceived, but the woman being deceived, fell into transgression. **15**But women will be preserved through the bearing of children if they continue in faith and love and sanctity with self-restraint.

Praying in Peace (2:8)

In the previous section (1 Timothy 2:1–7), Paul called for prayers for the salvation of everyone. Here Paul opens with "therefore" (1 Tim. 2:8), tying this passage on prayer to his prior instructions. His reasoning flowed like a smooth river: "Therefore," while on the subject, as the people gather to pray, be sure the meetings don't degrade into angry disputes.[1]

In contrast to women, who will be given instruction in the next section, Paul was addressing Ephesian men who were involved in prayer-time disputes. "In every place" is a reference to all of the house churches gathering in and around Ephesus (2:8). The dissension within the church was created by the Ephesian false teachers. They were full of strange doctrines (1:4–8) that brought about much speculation and fruitless disputes (see also 6:4).

The emphasis lies on the necessity that the men not be angry or contentious at times of prayer rather than on the specific form of the prayer—"lifting up holy hands." The posture of praying with the lifting of "holy hands" reflects the Old Testament requirement that hands be ritually clean before approaching God (Exodus 30:19–21; Psalm 24:4; Isaiah 1:15; 59:3). Later, this idea of "holy hands" became more moral than ritual in meaning (James 4:8). When prayers were offered with angry hearts rather than holy hands, the prayers lost their effectiveness.

Glittering Garments (2:9–10)

No tank tops. No spaghetti-straps. No short-shorts. No two-piece bathing suits. I recently read the rules for our church's youth camp. While many of them called for leaving iPods® and pranks at home, more than one rule related to modest attire. Like the church of the first century, the church of the twenty-first century must still give instructions on dressing modestly. If you have visited a college campus recently, you realize today's fashion trends include body piercing, bare midriffs, and shorter-than-ever-shorts. The youth camp rules are crowded with dress codes because the students in the youth group have a tendency to yield to contemporary trends that have long left modesty behind.

Paul wasn't writing rules for youth camp, but he was admonishing Christian women to dress in a godly and reserved fashion. Some of the women in the Ephesian churches had focused more on good looks as defined by their culture than they had on a godly life. Paul called for them to dress in a way that both reflected their Christian character and shifted their focus to doing good deeds that were even more becoming. Like the wise sage who declared, "Charm is deceitful and beauty is vain" (Proverbs 31:30), Paul also realized that external beauty fades fast.

While Paul criticized braided hair, gold, pearls, and costly garments in particular, we would do well to realize that the timeless truth of the passage is that modest dress is appropriate for godly women. The Ephesian false teachers may, in fact, have encouraged seductive and extravagant dress among the women in the church. Paul's statements here were a rebuttal to the opponents' call for attention-grabbing garments (2:9–10). The opponents were also teaching the widows to abstain from marriage (1 Tim. 4:3). Paul's desire for the young widows to remarry and have children was an indication that the false teachers had discounted the value of family relationships (5:14).

Compare Paul's comments in 1 Corinthians with those in 1 Timothy. In both Ephesus and Corinth, there were erroneous ideas about the wives' relationships with their husbands (1 Tim. 5:13–14; 1 Corinthians 11:2–16; 14:34–36). The false teachers may have been asserting that since God's kingdom had arrived, God's people were no longer subject to some aspects of creation—gender distinctions and sexual relationships (4:3). These ideas possibly came from misinterpreting some of Paul's own conclusions, such as: (1) "there is neither male nor female" in Christ (Galatians 3:28); and (2) remaining single is sometimes to be preferred over marriage (1 Cor. 7). Paul was trying to correct this false teaching, which had assumed that God's people were no longer living in the here and now. Paul reasserted creation and created order and the ongoing importance of role distinctions between men and women, distinctions that he saw rooted in creation.[2]

What does the Bible say about a woman preaching or teaching?

If 1 Timothy 5:1–11 is taken into account, we can also see that the false teachers in Ephesus were misleading the widows to such an extent that Paul attempted to rescue them from the clutches of his opponents. The rescue included proper dress, proper demeanor in worship, and accepting the possibility that they might get married and bear children. Given the women's excessive dress practices referred to in 2:9, some scholars have argued that these women were quite wealthy, thus making them a target for the false teachers' greed.

We can also tie family relationships to Paul's call for modesty when we realize that extravagant and immodest dress was often associated with marital infidelity and lewd living. The issue was not so much the specific hairstyle or jewelry, but the appearance of immorality. Above all else, Paul wanted the Ephesian women to place a priority on godly living. Paul emphasized "good works" in both 2:10 and 5:10–11, where widows were recognized for their "good works."

> *Back home . . . she would have never considered preaching from the pulpit a possibility.*

Throughout his letters, Paul emphasized that good deeds are the real result of a saving relationship with Christ Jesus (Romans 2:6–7; 13:3; 2 Corinthians 9:8; Ephesians 2:10; Philippians 1:6; Colossians 1:10; 2 Thessalonians 2:17). The opponents' false doctrines were leading to lives of immorality and to evil and wicked deeds.

Words from Women (2:11–15)

Before we address our specific passage, let us consider several overall assertions from Paul's teaching elsewhere. Numerous passages make clear that women can be excellent teachers:

- Older women were told to teach younger women (Titus 2:3–5).
- Timothy had learned his faith from his mother and grandmother (2 Tim. 1:5; 3:15).
- Priscilla, along with her husband Aquila, taught Apollos (Acts 18:26).
- All believers were to teach one another (Colossians 3:16).
- In other churches, women were allowed to prophesy (1 Corinthians 11:5).
- Paul acknowledged Philip's four daughters who prophesied (Acts 21:8–9).

We must remember that Paul was writing in the first century, when cultural conditions in both Judaism and elsewhere did not permit a woman to teach a man. While Paul also addressed slavery in the first century (Col. 3:22), that does not mean that Paul would support slavery in the twenty-first century. Paul wrote within the cultural conditions of his day. We cannot expect Paul to have written with regard to twenty-first century concerns when he lived in the first century.

Would she stand and preach or sit silently?

Overwhelmingly, Paul lifted women up in a culture that tended to push them down (Gal. 3:28). Paul greatly respected Priscilla (Acts 18:2, 18, 26; Rom. 16:3; 1 Cor. 16:19; 2 Tim. 4:19). Lydia was crucial to his ministry in Macedonia (Acts 16:14, 40). Phoebe was "a deacon at the church of Cenchreae"

(Rom. 16:1, NRSV), and Euodia and Syntyche were called Paul's "fellow workers" (Philippians 4:2–3).

Paul was so positive about the role of women that it created problems in unexpected ways. Therefore, when Paul addressed women or wives he was often correcting those who had applied his teachings in such a way as to offend cultural traditions. His writings might have sounded like: *I didn't mean for you to reject your husbands or upset the whole household. Your domineering over your husband will not be a good testimony* (paraphrase of ideas found in 1 Cor. 7 and Ephesians 5:21–33).

Having set the stage by acknowledging Paul's positive position in regard to women, especially in comparison with other teachers of his day, I am going to set forth my understanding of the meaning of this passage, realizing there are other valid interpretations.

When prayers were offered with angry hearts rather than holy hands, the prayers lost their effectiveness.

Paul called for women to sit quietly and learn with a submissive spirit (1 Tim. 2:11). Again, the situation with the Ephesian women seems to parallel the situation with the women in Corinth (compare 1 Cor. 14:34–35). The passage to the Corinthians clearly deals with a woman's demeanor in public worship. This was probably also the case in Ephesus. The Ephesian women (and the Corinthian women) had found new freedom in the gospel and had taken advantage of their emancipation by loudly lording it over men. Excessively breaking with the cultural norm, these women brought condemnation on the whole church. Therefore, Paul called for the overbearing Ephesian women to listen "quietly" in public worship (1 Tim. 2:11).

The Ephesian women were falling prey to the influence of Paul's opponents. Some commentators argue that Paul was talking about husbands and wives in this passage. However, the broader concern in 1 Timothy for widows demonstrates that he was most likely addressing men and women (5:9–13).

When Paul called for the women to be quiet, we must put that against the Ephesian setting where some women were talkative busybodies (5:13). Likewise, in 1 Thessalonians, he called on all church members—both men and women—to live quietly and mind their own affairs and work with their hands (1 Thess. 4:11; see also 2 Thess. 3:12). In fact, although other people discouraged Jewish women from learning, Paul was actually including them in the circle of students. Even though Paul called for these "busybody women" to receive instruction with submissiveness, we must also recognize that Paul never called on all women to be submissive to all men (see Titus 2:5; 1 Peter 3:5). Rather, it is most likely that Paul was calling the women to be submissive to the teaching overseers, those who were responsible for teaching the truth and

> *. . . The timeless truth of the passage is that modest dress is appropriate for godly women.*

correcting Paul's opponents. Paul was addressing a specific, historical situation in Ephesus.

Corresponding to Paul's assertion that a woman should learn is his statement, "I do not allow a woman to teach" (1 Tim. 2:12). False teachers were at the center of the problem in Ephesus (1:3; 6:3). Because these opponents had specifically led women astray in the house churches, Paul wanted to prohibit the women's involvement with spreading false teaching.

The issue was not so much the specific hairstyle or jewelry, but the appearance of immorality.

Therefore, Paul concluded that, instead of teaching, women were "to remain quiet" and thus learn with a quiet demeanor. The Greek text is best translated here "in a quiet demeanor" rather than "keep silent" (2:12, NRSV) or "be silent" (NIV). (See also 1 Thess. 4:11; 2 Thess. 3:12; and 1 Peter 3:4, where the same word group is used.) Elsewhere, we know that Paul permitted women to prophesy (1 Cor. 11:5), and he clearly acknowledged Priscilla's role along with Aquilla in instructing Apollos (Acts 18:26).

Therefore, these busybody Ephesian women were allowed to learn, but they could not get involved in teaching. Eve was representative, for the purposes of Paul's present argument, of the women in Ephesus who were led astray.[3] As Eve was fooled by the deceiver, the Ephesian women were being tricked by Paul's opponents (1 Tim. 4:3; 5:11–15; 2 Tim.3:5–9).

Our final verse presents one of the most difficult expressions in all of the pastoral epistles: "women will be preserved through the bearing of children" (1 Tim. 2:15). Some have taken this to mean that women will get safely through childbirth, reflecting the story in Genesis 3 of Adam and Eve's sin (see Genesis 3:16). Others see the childbirth as a reference to Mary's giving birth to Jesus. Most likely, however, Paul was reflecting on the good deeds that flow from a godly woman. Such deeds, despite the teaching of the opponents to the contrary, included marrying, bearing children, and being a godly wife and mother. Thus the interpretation of the passage should be set in the context of the false teachers who were opposing Paul and his gospel at Ephesus. Salvation, for Paul, is always based on faith in Christ (Eph. 2:8).

. . . Paul was writing in the first century, when cultural conditions in both Judaism and elsewhere did not permit a woman to teach a man.

When understood within the context of the Ephesian heresy, Paul's statements become clearer. Paul intended for Timothy to restrict these runaway women in Ephesus but never placed these restrictions into a command for all times and all places. Above all else, the men were to pray in such a way as to avoid dissension while the women were to live godly lives and focus their energy on bearing the fruit of good deeds rather than on outer adornment.

Teacher of Men

My love for the Greek New Testament was given to me by my first professor of New Testament Greek, a woman at a very conservative Baptist seminary. She, with great skill and humility of heart, taught a large class of mostly men how to read Paul's New Testament letters—including our present passage—from the original language. Ironically, many Baptist pastors would not be able to read in the original language Paul's prohibitions against a woman teaching had they not been taught by this woman. While the seminary allowed women to teach as "instructors" in theology classes, it was slow to offer them tenure track positions. The irony of such inconsistency was apparent to many students.

Questions

1. Why are churches sometimes inconsistent with regard to women in teaching ministries? Why might a woman be permitted to teach on the mission field but not at her own country?

2. How much of Paul's admonition against women teachers was based on the Ephesian context?

3. How can we apply Paul's continued emphasis against disputes and fruitless discussions to today's church?

4. How can we teach our students to dress modestly when clothing trends and role models in the entertainment world tend to encourage dress that depicts young girls as sex objects?

NOTES

1. Gordon D. Fee, *1 and 2 Timothy, Titus*, New International Biblical Commentary (Peabody, MA: Hendrickson Publishers, 1988), 71.
2. William D. Mounce, *Pastoral Epistles*, Word Biblical Commentary (Nashville: Thomas Nelson Publishers, 2000), 111.
3. Please note in Genesis 3:17 that it is not the woman who is blamed for eating the fruit, but the man.

Main Idea

Church servant leaders are
to be people of high spiritual
qualifications who care
faithfully for God's church
and represent it well.

Question to Explore

What kind of leaders
does a church need?

July 23

Aug 20

LESSON FOUR

Worthy Church Leaders

Study Aim

To summarize the instructions
about church leaders and
evaluate our church's leadership
pattern by these instructions

Study and Action Emphases

- Affirm the Bible as our authoritative guide for life and ministry
- Develop a growing, vibrant faith
- Include all God's family in decision-making and service
- Value all people as created in the image of God
- Encourage healthy families
- Equip people for servant leadership

Quick Read

Paul carefully described the qualities desired in church leaders. By living Christlike lives, church leaders could help restore the gospel's reputation, which had been tarnished by the boisterous living of the Ephesian false teachers.

Much confusion exists about church leadership. Paul's present passage will not answer all of our questions, but careful consideration of 1 Timothy 3:1–13 will offer us some clarity.

1 Timothy 3:1–13

1It is a trustworthy statement: if any man aspires to the office of overseer, it is a fine work he desires to do. **2**An overseer, then, must be above reproach, the husband of one wife, temperate, prudent, respectable, hospitable, able to teach, **3**not addicted to wine or pugnacious, but gentle, peaceable, free from the love of money. **4**He must be one who manages his own household well, keeping his children under control with all dignity **5**(but if a man does not know how to manage his own household, how will he take care of the church of God?), **6**and not a new convert, so that he will not become conceited and fall into the condemnation incurred by the devil. **7**And he must have a good reputation with those outside the church, so that he will not fall into reproach and the snare of the devil.

8Deacons likewise must be men of dignity, not double-tongued, or addicted to much wine or fond of sordid gain, **9**but holding to the mystery of the faith with a clear conscience. **10**These men must also first be tested; then let them serve as deacons if they are beyond reproach. **11**Women must likewise be dignified, not malicious gossips, but temperate, faithful in all things.

12Deacons must be husbands of only one wife, and good managers of their children and their own households. **13**For those who have served well as deacons obtain for themselves a high standing and great confidence in the faith that is in Christ Jesus.

Observation of Overseers (3:1–7)

While the list of qualifications for an "overseer" (1 Timothy 3:1) in the church might seem somewhat random at first glance, we must remember that the number one problem plaguing the Ephesian churches was a leadership crisis created by Paul's opponents. Choosing good pastors (over-seers) for the churches was of primary importance. Overseers were responsible for the administration and teaching within the church while deacons dealt with the day-to-day needs of serving

> *Choosing good pastors (overseers) for the churches was of primary importance.*

church members. Overseers, therefore, needed both management and teaching skills. Overseers are sometimes called "elders" in the New Testament (see Acts 20:17, 28; Titus 1:5, 7 where the terms are used interchangeably).

While we wish that Paul had given us both the qualifications and duties of overseers, this list concerns itself only with qualifications, especially outward, measurable behavior. This focus on outward actions was a reaction to the boisterous behavior of the false teachers, who had embarrassed both the church and the gospel. By setting forth these measurable qualifications, Paul was also giving the church standards by which to both evaluate and remove overseers/elders who were not living "up to code."

Overseers were responsible for the administration and teaching within the church while deacons dealt with the day-to-day needs of serving church members.

Studying the list of qualities, we can make a few observations about the duties of the overseers/elders. Unlike deacons, they were required to be able to teach (1 Tim. 3:2). This was especially important because false teaching was a primary problem in Ephesus. Also, unlike Paul's opponents, who demonstrated a tendency toward greed, both overseers and deacons had to take care in managing the church's money (3:3, 8). This may be an indication that overseers and deacons shared responsibility for church finances. The overseers, moreover, were also responsible for hospitality, for providing housing for visiting Christians (3:2).

Before Paul set forth these particulars for pastors (overseers), he gave his second "trustworthy statement" (see 1:15 for his first "trustworthy statement"). Using this "trustworthy statement" formula, Paul reinforced the importance of what was to follow. Paul encouraged prospective leaders by declaring that those who had an interest in the office of overseer were aspiring to a good work. Because of leadership abuses committed by Paul's opponents, perhaps potential overseers/elders were shunning leadership roles to avoid association or confrontation with the opponents.

Before Paul turned to specific requirements, he made certain that the overseers understood that— above all else—they were to never bring reproach on the church (3:2). Paul's opponents were dragging down the church's reputation. However, a true overseer (elder, pastor) would help the church regain its good standing in the community.

The false teachers had tried to make the gospel a personal profit center (6:5). . . .

Expanding on this general call for Christlike living, Paul set forth eleven attributes and three specific concerns for elders.

"Husband of one wife" (3:2). As Paul pressed out what it meant to be "above reproach" (3:1), he stated that the overseer should be, literally translated, a *one-woman man.* Unlike the opponents who had forbidden marriage (4:3) and who had been involved in sexual promiscuity (see 2 Timothy 3:6), Paul was proposing that the overseer/elder live as a faithful husband. Given the first place position of the *one-woman-kind-of-man* requirement, we can infer that marital faithfulness was a serious issue in the Ephesian churches.

Paul's words have been interpreted in various ways. Paul was saying that an overseer/elder (1) must be married, or (2) must be married to only one wife (no polygamy), or (3) cannot be remarried after death or divorce ended his first marriage, or (4) must remain faithful to his wife. The first interpretation is unlikely because Paul and Timothy were probably not married, and elsewhere we know that Paul held high the status of singles (see 1 Corinthians 7). The emphasis of the passage, moreover, is on *one* wife and not on marital status itself. Also, because polygamy was not a serious problem within the Christian community, the second interpretation seems amiss.

Paul encouraged prospective leaders by declaring that those who had an interest in the office of overseer were aspiring to a good work.

The most probable interpretation of the passage asserts that the elders were to remain committed to their wives. Elaborating on what it means to be "above reproach," Paul called on overseers to avoid any appearance of immorality. This interpretation would not rule out the possibility that the overseer might remarry after the death of his spouse. A similar expression, *one-man woman*, is later used in this letter in regard to the widows in the church (1 Tim. 5:9). The expression in that case also does not seem to rule out remarriage (5:14).

"Temperate, prudent, respectable" (3:2). "Temperate" carries the idea of clear-mindedness, exerting self-control over rash actions. "Prudent" may contain the idea of sexual decency (see Titus 2:5). "Respectable" relates to a person's outward appearance and balances off "prudent," which describes an inner quality. When this word is used elsewhere in the New Testament it addresses the description of a

woman's clothing (2:9; the word is used only these two times in the New Testament).

"Hospitable" (3:2). Overseers should gladly welcome fellow believers into their homes. The development of hospices and hospitals was an outgrowth of hospitality. The sending and receiving of guests, especially traveling teachers, was important in the early church (Romans 12:13; Hebrews 13:2; 1 Peter 4:9).

"Able to teach" (3:2). The overseer/elder must be able to both teach the truth and refute error. Paul later asserted that the elders who labored in teaching were to receive "double honor" (1 Tim. 5:17). The ability to teach set the overseers apart from the deacons who were to serve. The overseers/elders were teachers and administrators, while the deacons were involved in the day-to-day service in the church. Paul's opponents were not faithful teachers; they were teaching a different gospel (1:4). Timothy and the overseers/elders, in contrast, were to teach the true gospel (4:13; 2 Tim. 2:2).

> *The New Testament may demonstrate a two-step process for how church leadership developed over time.*

"Not addicted to wine" (3:3). The fact that this requirement is repeated for deacons may suggest that drunkenness was a serious problem in the Ephesian church (1 Tim. 3:8). While the false teachers had been overly prudent with respect to food (4:3), they seemed to have been given to drunkenness. Drinking is mentioned again in 5:23 as Paul encouraged Timothy

to use a little wine for medicinal purposes. Timothy might have totally abstained from alcohol because of its overuse within the church (5:23). In the New Testament, drunkenness is, without exception, pictured as an evil (Matthew 11:19; 24:49; Acts 2:15; 1 Corinthians 11:21; Ephesians 5:18; 1 Thessalonians 5:7). It often appears in lists of sins (Luke 21:34; Romans 13:13; 1 Cor. 6:10; Galatians 5:21; 1 Peter 4:3).

Not "pugnacious, but gentle" and uncontentious (3:3). Unlike a brawling drunkard, the elders were to be "gentle" or *not violent*. They were to be gracious and not quarrelsome. The description of the opponents makes clear that they were especially given to meaningless arguments (6:3–5; 2 Tim. 2:22–26).

"Free from the love of money" (3:3). This description is repeated for the deacons (1 Tim. 3:8). The false teachers had tried to make the gospel a personal profit center (6:5) and had been lovers of money (2 Tim. 3:2).

Those who were faithful in their service as deacons obtained "a high standing and great confidence in the faith that is in Christ Jesus" (1 Tim. 3:13).

Having set forth these eleven particulars for pastors/overseers, Paul addressed three final concerns. The church leader must: (1) manage his household in an exemplary fashion (3:4); (2) not be a new convert (3:6); and (3) be a person with a good reputation outside the church (3:7). The New Testament often depicts the church as family or even "the household of God" (3:15), thus emphasizing the relationship between the church and home. If overseers/elders failed at governing their own family, how could they possibly lead the family of God? Paul was also concerned that the overseer/elder not be "a new convert" (3:6), literally *newly planted*. A new believer might become arrogant when given too much responsibility, thus falling into the prideful sin of Satan. The devil was judged because of the arrogance he demonstrated toward God (Jude 9).

Description of Deacons (3:8–13)

Paul turned his attention to a different segment of church leadership, called "deacons" (1 Tim. 3:8) The New Testament may demonstrate a two-step process for how church leadership developed over time. At first, the apostles alone were leading the church in Jerusalem. As time passed, however, they were unable to meet all of the needs of the growing membership. Seven men, therefore, were appointed to serve (Acts 6:1–6, although that text does not use the word *deacon*). Likewise, at the end of his first missionary journey (Acts 14:23) and his preaching in Crete (Titus 1:5–9), Paul first appointed overseers—not deacons—in these young churches. In the more established churches of Philippi (Philippians 1:1) and Ephesus (1 Tim. 3:8–13), however, we find both overseers (leaders) and deacons (helpers). The office of deacon developed, perhaps, on a church-by-church basis as needs increased with church growth.[1]

Much like the list regarding the overseers, the list of qualities for the deacons does not include a clear explanation of duties. Likewise, as Paul opened with a broad description of the overseer ("beyond reproach") and then followed with specific attributes, Paul used a similar pattern—general to specific—when describing the qualities desired of a deacon. Deacons, primarily, were to be "men of dignity" (3:8, *worthy of respect*). Of the nine characteristics desired of a deacon, six of them closely parallel the characteristics for an overseer: dignified, not a drunkard, not greedy, blameless ("above reproach"), *one-woman man*, and a good manager of one's household.

Unlike the overseer, however, the deacon was not required to teach. Also, no mention is made of hospitality, suggesting that deacons were not responsible for the housing of itinerant preachers. The deacon (servant), as the title implies, was responsible for meeting the day-to-day needs of church members. While the overseer/elder and the deacon share many attributes, they were two distinct offices in the early church.

In addition to the qualifications shared with overseers, the deacons were also described by three additional attributes.

"Not double-tongued" (3:8). Paul was indicating that the deacon should not gossip, should not say one thing while actually meaning another, and should not say one thing to one person and something else to another.

"Holding to the mystery of the faith with a clear conscience" (3:9). The wayward leaders in Ephesus had shipwrecked their faith and already branded their consciences (1:19). Deacons, however, were to have a firm grasp on "the mystery of the faith," on the gospel. Their consciences should not be tainted by carrying the guilt of unconfessed sin.

Let these "also first be tested" (3:10). Perhaps Paul was suggesting a formal examination that considered a candidate's background, reputation, and understanding of the gospel. This examination might have involved a probationary period. The overseers were probably involved in evaluating the deacons since they had been given the responsibility for general oversight and for rebuking errors (Titus 1:9).

Those who were faithful in their service as deacons obtained "a high standing and great confidence in the faith that is in Christ Jesus" (1 Tim. 3:13). Paul indicated that those who were faithful gained influence and reputation within the believing community. He might also have been referring to their standing before God.

Words to the Women (3:11)

The word translated "women" can mean either *wives* or *women*. Unfortunately, it is not clear whether Paul was addressing the wives of the deacons or addressing a third, distinct group of officers, deaconesses. The feminine form of the word *deacon* had not yet been used in Greek language. In fact, in Romans 16:1, Phoebe was called a *deacon*, using the masculine form of the word.

Regardless of whether Paul was referring to the deacon's wife or a separate order of deaconesses, women helped greatly with service in the early church, and deaconesses appeared very early in church history.[2] Several indications make it probable that Paul was addressing a different category of church leaders. For example, when he switched from elders to deacons he used the Greek construction "deacons likewise" (3:8). In verse 11, he used a similar Greek construction, "women likewise." The parallel use of "likewise" in both cases (3:8 and 3:11) suggests Paul was repeating his formula for introducing a new category of church leaders. If Paul were addressing the wife of the deacon, moreover, we would have expected a word about the wife of the overseer in the previous address. If it is a new category, however, it does seem strange that Paul's address to them is sandwiched within his address to deacons.

Conclusion

Because the behavior of Paul's opponents had harmed the reputation of the church, Paul set forth the measurable qualities desired in church leaders. Paul called for overseers/elders to live "above reproach" (3:2) and deacons and deaconesses (or deacons' wives) to be people of unquestionable character.

Divorced Deacons?

Because many readers interpret Paul's *one-woman man* (1 Tim. 3:2, 12) to mean that divorce is never acceptable for a deacon, some churches refuse to allow someone who has experienced divorce to ever serve in the office of deacon. Other churches readily welcome divorced people to serve as deacons without asking any questions regarding the circumstances of their failed marriage. Both of these extremes, however, seem simplistic to me.

Under certain circumstances, someone could be divorced, even remarried, and still keep Paul's admonition to be faithful to the one's spouse. Deacon selection committees should carefully investigate the circumstances surrounding a deacon candidate's divorce. What was involved? Abandonment of a spouse by the candidate? Adultery on the candidate's part? While churches should exclude people in these circumstances from serving as deacons, other circumstances might allow someone to serve. What if the spouse abandoned the candidate? What if the candidate remained faithful despite the spouse's unfaithfulness? What if the divorce occurred before the candidate became a follower of Christ? What if the candidate has now demonstrated many years of faithfulness to the present spouse?

Simplistic answers rarely solve complicated problems. Churches must have the courage to deal confidentially on a case by case basis with each deacon candidate who has been divorced.

Questions

1. Having studied the separate lists of qualifications for overseers/elders and deacons, what conclusions can we draw about their respective duties?

2. Should people seek leadership roles in the church for themselves or should the church take the initiative in leadership selection?

3. When we look at Paul's lists of qualifications for leaders, what can we conclude about Paul's opponents?

4. When do women best meet the ministry needs of other women?

5. When do men best meet the ministry needs of other men?

NOTES

1. Robert Mounce, *Pastoral Epistles*, Word Biblical Commentary (Nashville: Thomas Nelson Publishers, 2000), 175.
2. Mounce, 202.

Main Idea

We are to grow toward becoming robust, vigorous Christians.

Question to Explore

How can we become robust, vigorous Christians?

LESSON FIVE

Toward Robust Christian Living

Study Aim

To identify specific ways for living a robust Christian life and decide on at least one I will put into practice

Study and Action Emphases

- Affirm the Bible as our authoritative guide for life and ministry
- Develop a growing, vibrant faith
- Equip people for servant leadership

Quick Read

Paul thought that Timothy should not be surprised by the fact that some church members were following the false teachers' spurious doctrines of purity. To counter the opponents, Timothy was to preach the gospel and exercise spiritual training in godliness like an athlete preparing for competition.

A man was being tailgated by another driver on a busy boulevard. Suddenly, the light turned yellow, and he put on the brakes. The tailgater blasted the horn, screamed in frustration, and made lewd gestures to the safe driver.

In the middle of the tirade, the tailgater heard a tap on the window. A police officer ordered the tailgater out of the car. The tailgater was taken to the police station, fingerprinted, photographed, and placed in a holding cell.

After several hours, the police officer approached the cell, opened the door, and apologized. The officer said, "You see, I pulled up behind your car while you were blowing your horn, shaking your fist, and cursing a blue streak. I noticed the 'What Would Jesus Do?' bumper sticker, the 'Follow Me to Church' bumper sticker, and the chrome-plated fish emblem on the trunk. Naturally, I assumed you had stolen the car."

How we live really does make a difference!

1 Timothy 4:1–16

¹But the Spirit explicitly says that in later times some will fall away from the faith, paying attention to deceitful spirits and doctrines of demons, ²by means of the hypocrisy of liars seared in their own conscience as with a branding iron, ³men who forbid marriage and advocate abstaining from foods which God has created to be

gratefully shared in by those who believe and know the truth. **4**For everything created by God is good, and nothing is to be rejected if it is received with gratitude; **5**for it is sanctified by means of the word of God and prayer.

6In pointing out these things to the brethren, you will be a good servant of Christ Jesus, constantly nourished on the words of the faith and of the sound doctrine which you have been following. **7**But have nothing to do with worldly fables fit only for old women. On the other hand, discipline yourself for the purpose of godliness; **8**for bodily discipline is only of little profit, but godliness is profitable for all things, since it holds promise for the present life and also for the life to come. **9**It is a trustworthy statement deserving full acceptance. **10**For it is for this we labor and strive, because we have fixed our hope on the living God, who is the Savior of all men, especially of believers.

11Prescribe and teach these things. **12**Let no one look down on your youthfulness, but rather in speech, conduct, love, faith and purity, show yourself an example of those who believe. **13**Until I come, give attention to the public reading of Scripture, to exhortation and teaching. **14**Do not neglect the spiritual gift within you, which was bestowed on you through prophetic utterance with the laying on of hands by the presbytery. **15**Take pains with these things; be absorbed in them, so that your progress will be evident to all. **16**Pay close attention to yourself and to your teaching; persevere in these things, for as you do this you will ensure salvation both for yourself and for those who hear you.

Falling Away from the Faith (4:1–5)

First, Paul did not want Timothy to be surprised that some of the Ephesian believers were falling away from the faith and following "the doctrines of demons" (1 Timothy 4:1). The Spirit had already forewarned about this. Second, Paul indicated that the source of his opponents' false teaching was no less than demonic.

In the closing verses of chapter 3, Paul made clear that the church had been entrusted with the gospel, the story of Jesus. Paul quoted an ancient hymn in 3:16. While the church was to hold on to the truth, Timothy should not be surprised that "in later times" some would abandon the faith. Some of the members of God's household (1 Tim. 3:15) were being led astray by the hypocritical liars, the false teachers in Ephesus (4:1–2; see also 2 Timothy 2:16–18; 3:13; 4:3–4).

When Paul wrote "the Spirit explicitly says" (1 Tim. 4:1), we are prompted to ask, *Where was this information found?* There is no Old Testament passage that exactly matches this message. When Paul referred to the Old Testament, moreover, he never used the formula "the Spirit explicitly says." When Paul himself—Spirit-inspired—addressed the elders of the Ephesian church, however, he had warned that there would be "savage wolves" who would come in among them and devour the flock (Acts 20:29). Paul had also written Spirit-inspired letters in which he had made predictions about coming defections (see 2 Thessalonians 2:1–11).

In addition to Paul's predictions, Jesus had also foreseen the emergence of false teachers (Matthew 24:11; Mark 13:22). Among the seven letters to churches found in Revelation 2—3, the one to Ephesus predicted the church's difficulty with false apostles (Revelation 2:2). This is what "the Spirit was saying to the churches" (Rev. 2:7). Paul, therefore, could have been referring to the teaching of Jesus, to his own statements or writings, or even unrecorded prophecies the Spirit had given to believers that had been communicated to the church.

When Paul said "in later times some will fall away" (1 Tim. 4:1), he was using Jewish language to describe the last days, which were to begin at the appearance of the Messiah. Jewish teachers spoke of the present evil age and the age to come (the last days). Even though Christians must still await the return of Christ to be fully in the new age, in the kingdom, we are already in the last days because the Messiah has appeared.

Paul wanted Timothy to realize that the battle in the Ephesian churches went beyond the opponents all the way back to the demonic powers who were at the heart of the false teaching. The role of Satan has already been touched on in 3:6–7 and will become apparent again in 2 Timothy 2:26. The opponents of Paul were hypocrites whose minds had been branded by Satan. Perhaps Paul said it best in Ephesians, "For our struggle is not against flesh and blood, but against the rulers, against the powers, against the world forces of this darkness, against the spiritual forces of wickedness in the heavenly places" (Ephesians 6:12).

Under the influence of evil powers, the false teachers were forbidding marriage and asking the believers to abstain from certain foods (1 Tim. 4:3). Marriage and food are related to our most basic physical appetites, sex and hunger.[1] Perhaps some young widows within the church had been influenced by the false teachers, who were persuading them not to remarry (5:11–15). These teachers taught that a celibate life put believers at a higher degree of holiness than a married life. They declared that the encumbering events of everyday life, including marriage and family life, were no longer acceptable because God's kingdom had arrived in Christ (compare 2 Thess. 2:1–2). This type of teaching came from a Greek idea that matter (that which is physical) was evil, and spirit (that which cannot be touched) was good. Such teaching espoused that sexual relations—even in marriage—were bad (1 Corinthians 7:1–7). Purity thus was achieved by avoiding marriage.

. . . Paul made clear that the church had been entrusted with the gospel, the story of Jesus.

The false teachers also asserted that the higher life included staying away from certain foods (see Colossians 2:21). Paul, on the other hand, generally argued that what a person ate made no difference (1 Cor. 8:8–9). Here he addressed the false teachers' call for abstinence from certain foods by saying that all that God has made is good (1 Tim. 4:3–5; Genesis 1:31). To reject certain foods because of ritual concerns is to somehow reject God's creative work (see Acts 10). We are to eat food with a heart of gratitude.

Jesus gave thanks while he fed the thousands (Matthew 14:19; 15:36; John 6:11) and as he gave thanks before distributing the bread at the Last Supper (Matt. 26:26–27; Mark 14:22–23). So we too are to give thanks for what God has provided for us. Food for Paul was a matter of conscience, and the one who abstains is not to judge another who eats (Romans 14:3, 10; 1 Cor. 10:29–30). By the act of thanksgiving, we have acknowledged God's creation of the food we enjoy.

We are to eat food with a heart of gratitude.

The call to abstain from marriage and certain foods, therefore, was not the teaching of the gospel but the "doctrines of demons" (1 Tim. 4:1). The Ephesian believers were not to be deceived by the false teachers.

Turning Toward Timothy (4:6–16)

Having focused on the nature of the errors of the false teachers, Paul turned toward Timothy's role as a teacher of the true gospel (1 Tim. 4:6, 11). Paul reminded Timothy that he had been nourished by the "words of the faith and of the sound doctrine" (4:6).

We discover at least three different sources of Timothy's being grounded in the faith. First, he received knowledge from his mother and his grandmother (2 Tim. 1:5; 3:14–15). Secondly, he had learned from experience in the church (Acts 16:2). Finally, he was Paul's son in the faith (1 Tim. 1:2). The pastoral epistles are often concerned with "sound teaching" (1:10; 2 Tim. 4:3; Titus 1:9, 2:1).

By the act of thanksgiving, we have acknowledged God's creation of the food we enjoy.

Paul stated that Timothy would be "a good servant of Christ Jesus" in pointing out these things (1 Tim. 4:6). "Pointing out these things" was the positive side of the instruction. The negative side was that Timothy "have nothing to do with worldly fables" (4:7). In contrast to "the words of the faith and the sound doctrine" (4:6), the teaching of the opponents was described as being *old wives' tales.* Their teaching was worthless.

In contrast, Timothy was to train himself for godliness (4:7). Continuing the athletic metaphor, Paul told Timothy that bodily exercise yields some temporary results, but spiritual discipline that leads to godliness yields results that last not only in this life but in the life to come. For Paul, eternal life has already begun for those who are in Christ Jesus. The life of the future is already a present reality for the people of God. As verse 8 states, "Godliness is profitable for all things since it holds promise for the present life and also for the life to come." In verse 9, we find Paul's third reference to a "trustworthy statement" (see 1:15; 3:1). The "trustworthy statement" most likely refers back to the end of verse 8, where godliness is valued.

Having set forth the statement in verse 8 and having declared the statement to be trustworthy in verse 9, Paul now gives us the reason in verse 10. The reason begins with "for." The verse could read, "For this [the present and future life that godliness promises] we labor and strive." The two verbs, "labor" and "strive," were favorites for Paul and often referred to his and others' ministries (compare Colossians 1:29, where they also occur together). The word "labor," referring to *a tiresome toil that requires our best effort*, has to do with competition (1 Tim. 6:12; 2 Tim. 4:7; 1 Corinthians 9:25) and thus carries the athletic theme forward from 1 Timothy 4:7. Godliness is not easily obtained. The word that means "strive" was also frequent with Paul and carries the idea of the marathon runner who is on his last ounce of energy as he tries to lean forward toward the finish line. Both of these verbs are used in the present tense, suggesting a continuous exertion of the Christian to strive for godliness.

> *. . . Spiritual discipline that leads to godliness yields results that last not only in this life but in the life to come.*

Just reading Lance Armstrong's training journal makes me tired! Weight training, four hours of bicycle riding, and uphill sprints exerting maximum effort were all part of his seven-day-a-week training routine as a cycling champion. How could anyone exert that much energy for that length of time? Like Armstrong's preparation for the Tour de France, Paul called for Christians to train, labor, and strive for godliness!

Paul called God "the Savior of all men, especially of believers" (1 Tim. 4:10). While some readers have tried to use this passage to promote universal salvation (everybody goes to heaven), the best translation understands the second phrase as repeating and clarifying the first. Paul was communicating that *God is the Savior of all people, that is, all who believe* (see 2 Tim. 4:13 and Titus 1:10 where "especially" is also used to clarify what is intended).

> *. . . Paul called for Christians to train, labor, and strive for godliness!*

By telling Timothy to "let no one look down on your youthfulness" (1 Tim. 4:12), Paul was offering the young man who was facing false teachers a word of encouragement. Timothy was probably thirty to thirty-five years of age and perhaps even timid (1 Cor. 16:10–11; 2 Tim.1:6–7). Young Timothy was living in a culture in which older people were highly regarded. Those under his charge would have been older than he was. Indirectly, Paul was also communicating to the church that—despite Timothy's young age—he operated under Paul's authority.

A college student from our church was performing a drama in a Russian orphanage, attempting to share the gospel in creative ways with the children. The Russian orphans were quick to make relationships and absorb every ounce of love offered to them. After the drama, children were allowed to ask questions. The first question was, "So, why are you here?" That question opened the door to share God's love with the children of Russia. Their next question was equally powerful, "Do you preach everywhere you go?"

Timothy was to serve as an example in every way imaginable—"in speech, conduct, love, faith and purity" (1 Tim. 4:12). The false teachers had abandoned faith and love (1:5–6) and had a false purity (4:3). Much like our summer missionary to Russia, Timothy was in every way and everywhere to preach the gospel. The Russian orphan asked the question, "Do you preach everywhere you go?" The answer is *Yes!* We are always carrying some message somewhere to someone. The call from Paul was for that message to be the gospel, to be carried by both our words and our actions.

Until Paul could arrive back on the scene, Timothy was to give special attention to the public reading of Scripture, to preaching, and to teaching (4:13). This list should probably not be taken as the pastor's specific duties in worship. Rather, they combine to represent the reading and explaining of Scripture. Calling Timothy not to neglect the gift he had been given, Paul was reminding him that he was foremost a preacher/teacher of the gospel. Through this role, he was to overcome the influence of the opponents and their false teaching (see also 2 Tim. 1:13–14; 2:15, 24–26; 3:14—4:5).

Paul made an interesting reference to "the laying on of hands" by the elders (see also 2 Tim. 1:6). Even in the Old Testament we find evidence of laying on of hands (Numbers 27:18–23; Deuteronomy 34:9). In Acts 13, the Spirit guides (Acts 13:2), the "prophets and teachers" are present (13:1), and the church lays on hands to consecrate those who are called (13:3). So, beginning in the earliest days, the church recognized gifts, prayed, and laid on hands to consecrate individuals to serve the greater community.[2]

"Do you preach everywhere you go?"

Finally, Paul closed by once again calling on Timothy to "pay attention" to both how he lived and what he taught and to approach both with a spirit of perseverance. Salvation for Paul always involved perseverance (2 Tim. 2:12; Col. 1:21–23a). By Timothy's example, the Ephesian believers were called to persevere in faith and love to their final destination—salvation.

Encouraging Others to Teach and Preach

In chapter 4, Paul encouraged Timothy to move forward in his faith and exert his spiritual gift of preaching and teaching. Following Paul's lead, our churches must both recognize and encourage those gifted for ministry. Unlike the false teachers who were asserting themselves, Timothy's gifts had been recognized by both Paul and the church. The call to ministry is a community event. Church members recognize the giftedness of others and encourage them to exercise their gifts within the community.

The example of George W. Truett's call clearly illustrates this role of the community. As a young man in Whitewright, Texas, Truett was repeatedly urged to become a minister. But he was adamant in his determination to be a lawyer. One Saturday in 1890, Truett attended a meeting at his church. He recalled, "When they got through with the rest of the church conference . . . the oldest deacon . . . rose up and began to talk. . . . 'There is such a thing as a church duty when the whole church must act. There is such a thing as an individual duty when the individual must face duty for himself. But it is my deep conviction as it is yours—that we have talked much one with another—that this church has a duty to perform and that we have waited late and long to get about it. I move, therefore, this church call a presbytery to ordain Brother George W. Truett to fulfill the work of the Gospel ministry.'"

Truett protested, imploring them to desist, but the church refused to hear his pleas. That Saturday the motion carried, the presbytery was summoned, and Truett was ordained.[3]

As Paul laid the burdens and joys of ministry on Timothy's shoulders, we, too, are to seek godly members who are called to serve.

Questions

1. How can we train ourselves with spiritual discipline?

2. Why do some people devote their energy to physical exercise, such as preparing to run a marathon, which promises only temporary results, and yet neglect spiritual exercise, such as Scripture reading and prayer, which yields eternal results?

3. Are any foods forbidden for followers of Christ today?

4. In what ways was Timothy to be an example to the Ephesian believers?

NOTES

1. John R. W. Stott, *The Message of 1 Timothy and Titus* (Downers Grove, IL: Inter-Varsity Press, 1996), 112.
2. For an extensive study on Baptists and ordination, see Howard K. Batson, "Pastoral/Lay Ministry Concerns in Ordination," *Baptists and Ordination*, William H. Brackney, Ed., (Macon, GA: The National Association of Baptist Professors of Religion, 2003), 157.
3. Batson, 161, citing Winthrop S. Hudson, "The Pastoral Ministry: Call and Ordination," *Foundations* 5 (1962), 242–243.

Focal Text
1 Timothy 6:2c–19

Background
1 Timothy 6:2c–21

Main Idea
Christians must emphasize godliness in contrast to seeking material wealth and use the wealth they have for God's purposes.

Question to Explore
How can we know when we value money too much?

LESSON SIX
Your Money or Your God

Study Aim
To summarize this lesson's teachings about material wealth and evaluate my view of material things by them

Study and Action Emphases

- Affirm the Bible as our authoritative guide for life and ministry
- Develop a growing, vibrant faith
- Obey and serve Jesus by meeting physical, spiritual, and emotional needs
- Equip people for servant leadership

Quick Read

Paul once again highlighted the impoverished teaching of his opponents and charged Timothy to stay faithful in his ministry until Christ returns. In response to the greedy false teachers, Paul emphasized the evil that results from loving money and seeking godless gain.

Gene was in the hospital, in the intensive care unit. He told the nurse to call his wife, Vernell, and ask her to bring his checkbook to the hospital. Vernell complied, although she thought it a most puzzling request.

"I want you to write out my tithe check," Gene said to his wife. "I've got to get it in this month. You write it, and I'll sign it."

Because of the oxygen mask, poor eyesight, and a lack of strength, it soon became clear that Gene could not accomplish the simple task of signing the check. Trying to reassure him, Vernell said, "Just don't worry about it. The church is not going to go under this month. We'll double up next month, and you'll be all caught up."

Before next month arrived, however, Gene died. Even before his funeral, his wife brought the "double tithe" check to the church office. The business administrator reined in his emotions as he received it.

The issue at hand was not money, but priorities. Even while hospitalized in the intensive care unit, Gene was concerned about his church, concerned about the work of God's kingdom. Gene was thinking about others, thinking about ministry, faithfulness, and priorities. At Gene's funeral, I held up the envelope that contained his last gift, a testimony to his priorities.

1 Timothy 6:2c–19

2 . . . Teach and preach these principles.

3If anyone advocates a different doctrine and does not agree with sound words, those of our Lord Jesus Christ, and with the doctrine conforming to godliness, **4**he is conceited and understands nothing; but he has a morbid interest in controversial questions and disputes about words, out of which arise envy, strife, abusive language, evil suspicions, **5**and constant friction between men of depraved mind and deprived of the truth, who suppose that godliness is a means of gain. **6**But godliness actually is a means of great gain when accompanied by contentment. **7**For we have brought nothing into the world, so we cannot take anything out of it either. **8**If we have food and covering, with these we shall be content. **9**But those who want to get rich fall into temptation and a snare and many foolish and harmful desires which plunge men into ruin and destruction. **10**For the love of money is a root of all sorts of evil, and some by longing for it have wandered away from the faith and pierced themselves with many griefs.

11But flee from these things, you man of God, and pursue righteousness, godliness, faith, love, perseverance and gentleness. **12**Fight the good fight of faith; take hold of the eternal life to which you were called, and you made the good confession in the presence of many witnesses. **13**I charge you in the presence of God, who gives life to all things, and of Christ Jesus, who testified the good confession before Pontius Pilate, **14**that you keep the commandment without stain or reproach until the appearing of our Lord Jesus Christ, **15**which He will bring about at the proper time—He who is the blessed and only Sovereign, the King of kings and Lord of lords, **16**who alone possesses immortality and dwells in unapproachable light, whom no man has seen or can see. To Him be honor and eternal dominion! Amen.

17Instruct those who are rich in this present world not to be conceited or to fix their hope on the uncertainty of riches, but on God, who richly supplies us with all things to enjoy. **18**Instruct them to do good, to be rich in good works, to be generous and ready to share, **19**storing up for themselves the treasure of a good foundation for the future, so that they may take hold of that which is life indeed.

A False Gospel for Godless Gain (6:1–5)

Throughout this letter we see two major concerns from the Apostle Paul: the false teachers and their fruitless debates; and Timothy's response. Once again, Paul called on his son in the faith to teach (1 Timothy 6:2c; see 1:3; 4:11). Paul had used "these principles" or "these things" throughout this letter (1 Tim. 6:2c; see 3:14; 4:6, 11; 5:7, 21) to indicate what had already been said. In this case, the reference may be to the material beginning in 2:1.

While false teachers were peddling false doctrine, Timothy was to teach the gospel as set forth by Paul (see also 1:3). Rejecting the opponents' false gospel, Paul called for Timothy to hold on to "sound words" (6:3; see also 1:10), "those of our Lord Jesus Christ." Paul was addressing either words spoken by Christ or words spoken about him, namely the preaching of the gospel as presented by Paul. We need not choose between these possibilities. Both are in harmony and teach the godliness Paul set forth as his goal (6:3).

The opponents were stirring up dissension and controversy rather than promoting sound (healthy) teaching. They had a morbid craving for controversial questions and disputes, literally promoting *word battles* (6:4). As a result, the church was left divided, disrupted, and disturbed.

At last, we discover the true motivation behind the folly of the false teachers. They were motivated by money (6:5). When previously describing the qualifications of both the overseer and the deacon, Paul asked the church to be certain to select officers who were not lovers of money (3:3, 8). He was guiding them away from people who were seeking godless gain. He knew that his opponents loved money. Preaching for profit was a problem then just as it is now (see 1 Thessalonians 2:5). Having revealed their godless greed, Paul now turned his attention to money matters.

Loving Money, Lurking Evil (6:6–10)

In this section, Paul set forth the perils of greed for gain, of loving money (6:10).

Loving money keeps us from seeing the brevity of the here and now (6:7). We each have a deep desire to collect, to make our own miniature museums, in this lifetime. Greed doesn't allow us to see that we are simply passing through this world. Advertisers know that if you start someone off with the first piece of a collection, then the person more likely will be driven to complete the whole set. Collecting pieces and parts of never-ending puzzles, we live as if we are going to be here forever.

A pastor made clear in one of his Sunday sermons that "the earth is the Lord's, and all it contains; The world, and those who dwell in it" (Psalm 24:1; see Exodus 9:29; Deuteronomy 10:14). Following the worship service, the pastor was invited to dine in the home of a wealthy parishioner. After lunch, the host suggested that they take a walk. Strolling through the parishioner's beautiful garden, the parishioner and the pastor looked across the fertile fields ripe with grain, admired his fine cattle, and then toured his huge barns. "Now, tell me," the man said, "are you really saying that these things don't belong to me?" The pastor replied, "Sir, ask me that question a hundred years from now."

"Now, tell me," the man said, "are you really saying that these things don't belong to me?"

Paul called the Ephesian churches to acknowledge the brevity of life (1 Tim. 6:7). Long before, Job had declared, "Naked I came from my mother's womb, and naked I shall return" (Job 1:21). In light of the reality that Christ is coming again for his people and that they will be able to take none of this world's goods with them, greed really makes no sense, and an emphasis on accumulating things thus is foolish.

Loving money leads to discontent (6:8). Modern marketing is based on the ploy of making us feel we are not whole unless we possess a particular product. If only you possessed the pizzazz that companies offered in their car, clothes, or cologne, then you would be a whole person. You would be more exciting, better looking, happier, and finally, at last, content. Advertisers cultivate needs by hitching their wares to the infinite yearnings of the human soul.

> *. . . The love of money leads us to be materialistic, shallow, self-centered people.*

Someone once said that you can never get enough of what you didn't want in the first place!

Humorist Erma Bombeck told about Christina, who had been diagnosed with cancer. A friend asked Christina what she would like for her eighth birthday. Christina rubbed her hands over her bald head, rested her face on her hands, and replied, "I don't know. I have two sticker books and a Cabbage Patch doll. I have everything!"[1] Paul agreed, "If we have food and covering, with these we shall be content" (1 Tim. 6:8).

Loving money leads to a landslide of sin (6:9–10). Greed can lead us to lie on our income tax return, covet our neighbor's new car, become bitter or resentful at someone else's easy gain, be envious of a sibling when we feel slighted in a will, become worshipers of work, and even skip church on Sunday in order to gain more goods. The number one cause of marital strife is fighting over finances! The prophet Malachi said we even rob God when we withhold our tithe (Malachi 3:8–12). Above all else, the love of money leads us to be materialistic, shallow, self-centered people. Amazingly, almost every sin is related, directly or indirectly, to the love of money.

> *Two dangers that face the rich are arrogance and a false sense of security based on fleeting wealth (1 Tim. 6:17).*

Our desire for material things sometimes makes us like people captured by the lust of the flesh. Instead of looking through pornographic magazines encouraging sins of sensuality, we window shop in the mall and peruse the pages of catalogs, gazing with greed at the many things of this world that arouse and encourage our materialistic fantasies.

Closing Commission to Timothy (6:11–16)

Paul's pattern in this book has been to expose the false teachers' bad behavior and faulty doctrine (1 Tim. 1:3–7, 18–20; 4:1–5) and then turn toward Timothy, calling on him to resist them and live the life of a godly teacher (1:3, 18–19; 4:6–16). In each of these appeals to Timothy, Paul touched on the beginning of Timothy's spiritual journey (1:18; 4:14; 6:12). Using four commands, Paul urged Timothy to avoid the sinful traps that had captured the false teachers and to continue his faithfulness in the true gospel until the last day (6:13–14). In charging Timothy, Paul also offered a beautiful doxology that is a rare jewel of praise found from the Apostle's pen (6:15–16).

Paul's four imperatives (commands) are clear (italics highlight the imperatives): (1) "*flee* from these things"; (2) "*pursue* righteousness, godliness, faith, love, perseverance and gentleness"; (3) "*fight* the good fight of faith"; and (4) "*take hold* of eternal life" (6:11–12).

First, Timothy was commanded to "*flee* from these things"—the love of money and the evil that accompanies such love (6:9–10). Second, he was to pursue six qualities, listed in pairs, that serve as an alternative to greed. In the third imperative, Timothy was called on to fight for, that is to *contend for*, the gospel, the story of Jesus. Fourth, Timothy was told to "*take hold* of eternal life." Paul was calling on this young disciple to live in the new age that had begun with Jesus' arrival.

In the midst of these imperatives, Paul called Timothy a "man of God," a title that contains many echoes from the Old Testament (see also 2 Timothy 3:17). In the Old Testament, this description was reserved for the choice servants of God, such as these: Moses (Deuteronomy 33:1; Joshua 14:6); David (Nehemiah 12:24); Samuel (1 Samuel 9:6); Elijah (1 Kings 17:18); and Elisha (2 Kings 4:7).

Flowing into verses 13–14, Timothy's final charge embodied within it a doxology that described both God and Jesus. God was called the One "who gives life to all things" (1 Tim. 6:13). Recalling Christ's courageous confession before Pilate, Paul encouraged Timothy to stand firm. Pilate claimed to have the power of life and death over Jesus. Our Lord reminded Pilate that he would have no power had it not been given to him by the One who controls all things (John 19:10–11).

Paul set forth the perils of greed for gain, of loving money (6:10).

Paul called Timothy to be obedient before the life-giving God and the confessional Christ. Timothy was to keep the commandment "without stain or reproach" until the return of Christ (1 Tim. 6:14). Timothy was to persevere in his faith and ministry (see 4:16). In turn, his steadfastness to the true gospel would be the best weapon against the false teachers.

Making mention of the return of Christ led Paul to a series of descriptions of God that are powerfully poetic. "King of kings" was used of Babylonian and Persian emperors (Ezekiel 26:7; Daniel 2:37; Ezra 7:12) but was later applied to God himself. In Deuteronomy 10:17 we find the use of "Lord of lords" to emphasize God's absolute power over all other gods or spiritual powers. These two terms were joined together to designate the Messiah (Revelation 17:14; 19:6) and emphasize God's total sovereignty over all.

Saying that God lives in "unapproachable light" recalls Psalm 104:2. There we are reminded of God's blinding glory, which no human eye can endure (Exodus 24:15–17; 34:29–35; 1 Kings 8:11).

A Final Word to the Wealthy (6:17–19)

I have conducted hundreds of funerals. Yet I have never witnessed a funeral procession in which the hearse was pulling a U-Haul trailer. We truly do leave everything behind when we die. Real, eternal riches come from treasures in the kingdom of God, the result of good deeds on behalf of the gospel.

Even before his funeral, his wife brought the "double tithe" check to the church office.

Two dangers that face the rich are arrogance and a false sense of security based on fleeting wealth (1 Tim. 6:17). Sometimes those who have acquired great wealth begin to think of themselves as smarter, more gifted, or more deserving of this world's riches than those around them. But wealth is always uncertain (Proverbs 23:4–5). At best, should we even remain wealthy our entire lifetime, we will lose all of our worldly wealth at death. Rather than seeing themselves as owners of riches, the wealthy should serve as stewards of God's good gifts, generous and ready to share (1 Tim. 6:18).

There is a familiar story about a man who made a vow to God and his pastor. He said, "If God will bless me, then I will unfailingly give a tithe of all my income to his work." He kept his vow at first, and business boomed, making his tithe more than $500 a week. Five dollars a week had been easy to give, and $50 was a delight, but $500 seemed an appalling sum. The man could think only of what he could do with the money if he spent it on himself and his family.

> Greed doesn't allow us to see that we are simply passing through this world.

The man went to his pastor and declared, "I simply cannot afford to tithe. I'm asking you to release me from my obligation." The pastor replied, "I'm sorry I cannot do that, but I tell you what I will do. Let's kneel down by my desk and we will ask the Lord to once again reduce your income enough so that you will feel that you are able to tithe again!"

Baptists have long taught that salvation cannot be earned. We must also realize that our deeds are judged (1 Corinthians 3:12–15) and that we are to lay up treasures for ourselves for the coming age (Matthew 6:19–21; see Luke 12:32–33).

As the Rich Get Richer, They Get More Stingy!

John and Sylvia Ronsvalle are considered by many to be leading experts on giving patterns of American Christians. They produce an annual report, *The State of Christian Giving.* They have been tracking the generosity—or lack thereof—of American Christians for three decades. Their recent report showed that the richer we become, the less we give in proportion to our incomes! Put plainly, poor and middle-class Christians give a larger portion of their income to the church than do the wealthy. More specifically, as we have become richer, we have chosen to spend more and more on ourselves and to give a smaller percentage to the church. The Ronsvalles concluded that if American Christians simply tithed, there would be another $143 billion available for the work of God's kingdom.[2]

Captivating Consumers

In 1986, Americans still had more high schools than shopping centers. Currently, however, we have twice as many shopping centers as we do high schools! We spend more on shoes, jewelry, and watches ($80 billion a year in the U.S. economy) than we do on higher education ($65 billion). Americans spend six hours a week shopping and only forty minutes a week playing with their children.

It can be argued that the mall is replacing the church as the center of American culture. Seventy percent of Americans visit shopping malls each week, which is considerably more than those who attend church. The shopping mall has become the gothic cathedral of the new culture of greed. Too, just as there are mega-churches, the mega-malls get bigger and bigger, with the Mall of America in Bloomington, Minnesota, employing 10,000 people! Shopping has become a form of entertainment to fill the void in our boring, meaningless lives.

Ironically, the more income rises across the board, the less we save. The more we make, the less we save because we have to upscale our lifestyle. Impoverished Chinese, Indian, and Pakistani workers actually save twenty-five percent of their incomes! Americans have been trapped by something called *spaving*. *Spaving* causes us to spend to save. You buy an item of clothing that was $200 and now it's just $100. Just think, you have *spaved* your family $100 by buying the clothing. If you don't buy it, you're not going to *spave* anything! American consumerism is out of control.[3]

Questions

1. Can you think of people who have considerable income but choose to live a modest lifestyle in order to share their wealth?

2. Why do American Christians give a smaller percentage of their income to the church when their income increases?

3. How many sins can you think of that relate to the love of money?

4. Is leaving a large inheritance to one's children always wise?

5. What do you need in order to be content?

NOTES

1. Erma Bombeck, *I Want to Grow Hair, I Want to Grow Up, I Want to Go to Boise* (New York City: Harper and Row Publishers, 1989), 7.
2. Ronald J. Sider, *The Scandal of the Evangelical Conscience* (Grand Rapids, MI: Baker House Books, 2005), 20–21.
3. John de Graaf, David Wann, Thomas H. Naylor, *Affluenza* (San Francisco: Berrett-Koehler Publishers, Inc., 2001), 4–25.

Introducing

2 TIMOTHY: A Legacy to Live By

As with 1 Timothy, 2 Timothy is identified as being from Paul to Timothy (2 Timothy 1:1–2). Rather than being a manual, a set of instructions, to use in guiding a church, this letter seems more to be like a "last will and testament." It has more of a personal touch and reads like a legacy being left by an older mentor to a younger person. The legacy includes encouragement ("be strong in the grace that is in Christ Jesus," 2 Tim. 2:1) as well as instruction ("what you have heard from me through many witnesses entrust to faithful people," 2:2).[1]

The lessons from 2 Timothy will encourage us to consider our own lives and our own legacy—both the legacy from which we are learning and the legacy we are leaving. Christians, of all people, need to learn the wisdom from experienced people of faith who are preceding them. They also need to learn to share their own faith stories with those who are following them. We do not travel this Way alone.

2 TIMOTHY: A LEGACY TO LIVE BY

Additional Resources for Studying 2 Timothy[2]

James D. G. Dunn. "The First and Second Letters to Timothy and the Letter to Titus." *The New Interpreter's Bible*. Volume XI. Nashville, Tennessee: Abingdon Press, 2000.

Gordon D. Fee. *1 and 2 Timothy*. New International Biblical Commentary. Peabody, Massachusetts: Hendrickson Publishers, 1988.

Donald Guthrie. *The Pastoral Epistles*. Revised edition. Tyndale New Testament Commentaries. Grand Rapids, Michigan: William B. Eerdmans Publishing Company, 1990.

E. Glenn Hinson. "1—2 Timothy and Titus." *The Broadman Bible Commentary*. Volume 11. Nashville, Tennessee: Broadman Press, 1971.

Thomas D. Lea and Hayne P. Griffin, Jr. *1, 2 Timothy, Titus*. The New American Commentary. Volume 34. Nashville, Tennessee: Broadman Press, 1992.

A. T. Robertson. *Word Pictures in the New Testament*. Volume IV. Nashville, Tennessee: Broadman Press, 1931.

Introducing 2 TIMOTHY: *A Legacy to Live By*

John R. W. Stott. *Guard the Gospel: The Message of 2 Timothy.* Downers Grove, Illinois: InterVarsity Press, 1973.

NOTES

1. Unless otherwise indicated, all Scripture quotations in this introduction and the lessons on 2 Timothy are from the New Revised Standard Version.
2. Listing a book does not imply full agreement by the writers or BAPTISTWAY PRESS® with all of its comments.

Main Idea

Shaping our lives in the best way calls for responding positively to the opportunities we have.

Question to Explore

What goes into the shaping of a life?

LESSON SEVEN

Shaping a Life

Study Aim

To recognize the ways in which my life is being shaped and to respond positively to the opportunities I have

Study and Action Emphases

- Affirm the Bible as our authoritative guide for life and ministry
- Share the gospel with all people
- Develop a growing, vibrant faith
- Encourage healthy families
- Equip people for servant leadership

Quick Read

Second Timothy is filled with encouragement and instruction for the Apostle Paul's "beloved child" in the ministry. This lesson considers the initial chapter of this letter, which is sometimes described as "Paul's last will and testament."

Taken together, 1 Timothy, 2 Timothy, and Titus are known as the pastoral epistles. Given this label for these letters, laypeople might well wonder how applicable and helpful these documents could possibly be for them. Although these letters are addressed to Timothy and Titus and are concerned with ministerial matters, the range of topics treated and the personal, practical nature of these epistles attract, encourage, and challenge laity as well as clergy. This is particularly true of 2 Timothy, which focuses less on church issues and more on Timothy's own faith commitment and development. Poignant, personal portraits of Paul also add color and interest to this letter.

Almost all of the Baptist churches with which I am acquainted value theological education, not only for their ministers but also for their members. Part of this educative process with respect to biblical studies is to recognize and even come to appreciate a diversity of interpretive viewpoints. When studying the pastoral epistles, it is both responsible and necessary to acknowledge that a large majority of contemporary Pauline scholars now consider these letters to have been written by one other than Paul. Some readers might find this idea threatening or perhaps even maddening. They may summarily dismiss such a preposterous, if not dangerous, proposal out of hand. Others will think this position intriguing, if not stimulating, and will choose to investigate the matter further.

Let me cut through the scholarly chase and state three options regarding authorship for your consideration. First, the traditional approach to these epistles is to presume their authenticity. With respect to 2 Timothy, it has historically been understood as a letter that Paul wrote to his junior colleague from his second Roman confinement in the middle 60s A.D. (see 2 Timothy 1:17). It has also typically been viewed as Paul's final letter. Second, as just stated, many Bible interpreters now regard the pastoral letters, including 2 Timothy, to have been written in Paul's name but not by Paul himself. On this view, the dating of the letter we are studying would fall sometime in the late first or early second century. Third, an articulate minority of Pauline scholars adopt a mediating position concerning authorship. Although they think the letters are after Paul's time, they maintain that the writer(s) of the letter(s) wove into the text authentic fragments written by the Apostle himself. This would be especially true, they contend, for 2 Timothy.

In this lesson, and the three that follow, I will simply refer to the author of 2 Timothy as Paul. Truth be told, strong cases have been, can be, and will be mounted both for and against the authenticity of 2 Timothy as a letter written by Paul. At present, academic certainty about the authorship of these letters is neither possible nor even necessary. Second Timothy is now a part of Christian Scripture and as such is "useful for teaching, for reproof, for correction, and for training in righteousness" (2 Tim. 3:16).

2 Timothy 1:1–14

1Paul, an apostle of Christ Jesus by the will of God, for the sake of the promise of life that is in Christ Jesus,

2To Timothy, my beloved child:

Grace, mercy, and peace from God the Father and Christ Jesus our Lord.

3I am grateful to God—whom I worship with a clear conscience, as my ancestors did—when I remember you constantly in my prayers night and day. **4**Recalling your tears, I long to see you so that I may be filled with joy. **5**I am reminded of your sincere faith, a faith that lived first in your grandmother Lois and your mother Eunice and now, I am sure, lives in you. **6**For this reason I remind you to rekindle the gift of God that is within you through the laying on of my hands; **7**for God did not give us a spirit of cowardice, but rather a spirit of power and of love and of self-discipline.

8Do not be ashamed, then, of the testimony about our Lord or of me his prisoner, but join with me in suffering for the gospel, relying on the power of God, **9**who saved us and called us with a holy calling, not according to our works but according to his own purpose and grace. This grace was given to us in Christ Jesus before the ages began, **10**but it has now been revealed through the appearing of our Savior Christ Jesus, who abolished death and brought life and immortality to light through the gospel. **11**For this gospel I was appointed a herald and an apostle and a teacher, **12**and for this reason I suffer as I do. But I am not ashamed, for I know the one in whom I have put my trust, and I am sure that he is able to guard until that day what I have entrusted to him. **13**Hold to the standard of sound teaching that you have heard from me, in the faith and love that are in Christ Jesus. **14**Guard the good treasure entrusted to you, with the help of the Holy Spirit living in us.

Salutation (1:1–2)

Paul began this letter to Timothy by describing himself as "an apostle of Christ Jesus" (1:1). This was a common self-description for Paul in the introduction to his letters (see Romans 1:1; 1 Corinthians 1:1; 2 Corinthians 1:1; Galatians 1:1; Ephesians 1:1; Colossians 1:1). Paul maintained that his apostleship was "by the will of God" on the one hand (see 1 Cor. 1:1) and "for the sake of the promise of life which is in Christ Jesus" on the other hand (see also 1 Tim. 4:8; 1 John 2:25).

Paul addressed Timothy as his "beloved child" (2 Tim. 1:2). Timothy, who often appeared as a co-sender in Paul's letters (note 2 Cor. 1:1; Philippians 1:1; Col. 1:1; 1 Thessalonians 1:1; 2 Thessalonians 1:1; Philemon 1), was named as the recipient of this letter (see also 1 Tim. 1:2). In Paul's letters, as well as in Acts, Timothy emerged as a trusted junior co-worker of the apostle's who played a pivotal role in his ministry (Rom. 16:21; 1 Cor. 4:17; 16:10; Phil. 2:19–24; 1 Thess. 3:2, 6; Acts 17:14–15; 18:5; 19:22; 20:4; see Hebrews 13:23). In fact, in Philippians 2,

Paul not only spoke of Timothy warmly as a "son" who had served alongside him in the gospel (Phil. 2:22), but he also informed the Philippian fellowship that he had "no one like him who will be genuinely concerned for [their] welfare" (Phil. 2:20).

. . . He had benefited from a godly ancestry and upbringing (see 2 Tim. 3:15).

By way of greeting, Paul extended to his valued ministerial colleague "grace, mercy, and peace from God the Father and Christ Jesus our Lord" (2 Tim. 1:2b). First Timothy is the only other Pauline letter that adds "mercy" to the typical "grace and peace" greeting.

Thanksgiving for Timothy (1:3–5)

In fine Pauline fashion, salutation transitions into thanksgiving. As elsewhere in Paul, there is an explicit link between giving thanks and praying to God on behalf of another—in this case Timothy (1:3; see Rom. 1:8–9; Phil. 1:3–5; Col. 1:3; 1 Thess. 1:2; Philemon 4).

Paul added the fascinating remark that he served God with a clear conscience as did his ancestors (2 Tim. 1:3). Some readers might be taken aback by Paul's claim that he, like his Jewish ancestors, had always lived his life with a clear conscience before God (see Acts 23:1; 24:16; Phil. 3:6). Paul apparently did not suffer pangs of conscience prior to his conversion and call. Paul would deeply regret his persecution of the church (1 Cor. 15:9; 1 Tim. 1:13), but he never indicated that he battled internal angst in his pre-Christian life. Interestingly, 1 Timothy considers a clear conscience to be a mark of Christian faith and service (1 Tim. 1:5, 19; 3:9).

Instead of shrinking back, Timothy, by relying on the power of God, was to exhibit a readiness and a willingness to suffer for the gospel (see 2:3).

As Paul prayed for Timothy by night and by day, he yearned to see him even as he recalled Timothy's tears (perhaps occasioned by their separation) and anticipated their joyful reunion (2 Tim. 1:4). Furthermore, praying for and thinking about Timothy prompted Paul to recall Timothy's spiritual heritage. The sincere faith that Paul was persuaded dwelt in Timothy first dwelt, Paul indicated, in Timothy's grandmother Lois and in his mother Eunice (1:5). Beyond the fact that Timothy's mother was a Jewish believer (Acts 16:1), we know nothing else about her, and this is the only existing literary reference to his grandmother Lois. What we may conclude from this verse, however, is that Timothy was not a spiritual *Johnny-come-lately*. Rather, he had benefited from a godly ancestry and upbringing (see 2 Tim. 3:15).

Instructions to Timothy (1:6–14)

Second Timothy is full of spiritual counsel from Paul to Timothy. Time and again Paul admonished

Timothy to embrace this thing or to exclude that thing. Such exhortations begin on the heels of the letter's introduction, and we encounter five admonitions in verses 6–14. Within these verses, Paul also engaged in theological reflection and personal confession (1:9–12).

First, because a sincere faith dwelt in Timothy, even as it had in his grandmother and mother, Paul reminded Timothy to "rekindle" (or *stir into flame*) "the gift of God that is within you through the laying on of my hands" (1:6). The gift of which Paul spoke appears to be the gift of ministry that God had entrusted to Timothy. The solemn, sacred occasion to which Paul referred does not constitute a formal ordination to ministry as we might now construe such. Rather, it connotes a commission to ministry and a reception of the Spirit's empowerment for ministry (see 1 Tim. 4:14). Indeed, in 2 Timothy 1:7 Paul stated that the Spirit that God gives is not typified by timidity or "cowardice." Rather, the Spirit of God is marked by, and marks believers with, "power" (or *boldness*), "love," and self-control.

> *. . . Praying for and thinking about Timothy prompted Paul to recall Timothy's spiritual heritage.*

Because God had given Timothy the empowerment of the Spirit, Paul enjoined Timothy not to be ashamed "of the testimony about our Lord" (1:8). In close relation, Paul called Timothy not to be embarrassed by his association with the Apostle, who was now imprisoned for the gospel (see 2:9). Instead of shrinking back, Timothy, by relying on the power of God, was to exhibit a readiness and a willingness to suffer for the gospel (see 2:3).

Mentioning God prompted Paul to speak of God's saving and sanctifying work on behalf of believers. Sounding a familiar refrain, Paul maintained that Christian salvation and calling result not from human exertion but from God's gracious purpose in Christ Jesus (1:9; see Rom. 3:24; Gal. 2:16; Eph. 2:8).

Regardless of our occupation, our Christian vocation is to live lives faithful to and unashamed of the gospel. . . .

Paul stated, "This grace was given to us in Christ Jesus before the ages began" (2 Tim. 1:9). Paul was emphasizing that Jesus was not a divine afterthought. By his appearing, Christ Jesus, the Savior, not only "abolished death" but also brought to light "life and immortality" (1:10).

In 1:11 Paul described himself as divinely commissioned to be a "herald," "apostle," and "teacher" of the gospel (see Gal. 1:11–12, 15–16). Part and parcel of this divine appointment, Paul contended, was the suffering that he experienced (2 Tim. 1:12). Far from novel, suffering typified the life of the Apostle, even as it marked the life of his Master (see 3:11; note also especially 2 Cor. 11:23–27). What is more, Paul regarded some degree of affliction and persecution as an integral and inevitable part of the Christian life (see 2 Tim. 3:12; 1 Thess. 3:4; Rom. 8:17; Phil. 1:29).

Suffering notwithstanding, Paul was "not ashamed" of the gospel (see Rom. 1:16). This fact reinforced his earlier exhortations to Timothy (see 2 Tim. 1:8). Paul was not merely admonishing Timothy. Rather Paul also was modeling the gospel for his child and colleague in ministry. In 1:12 Paul expressed his confidence in God to "guard" the gospel entrusted to him, and now to Timothy, until the time of Christ's coming (see 1 Tim. 6:20).

. . . Timothy was to pay diligent attention to the contents of the gospel, of which he was both a steward and a servant.

That being said, Paul also called Timothy to be trustworthy in his ministry (2 Tim.1:13–14). God is faithful and can be readily and fully trusted. We, too, are to be faithful in our gospel service (see 2:13). In so being, we image the divine. With respect to Timothy, Paul enjoined him to "hold to the standard of sound teaching that you have heard from me" (1:13). All the while, he was to do so "in the faith and love that are in Christ Jesus" (1:13). Instruction in the faith must be joined with incarnation of the faith. Not only are we to teach sound doctrine, but we are also to lead Christlike lives.

In the final verse in this lesson, Paul admonished Timothy to guard the "good treasure entrusted" to him (1:14). That is, Timothy was to pay diligent attention to the contents of the gospel, of which he was both a steward and a servant. In carrying out this spiritual responsibility, Timothy would not be left to his own resources and devices. On the contrary, he would be guided and directed through the Holy Spirit who dwelt in him and in all who have entrusted their lives to Christ.

Summary

Although 2 Timothy was not written to us, by virtue of the letter's inclusion in the New Testament canon we can consider it as divinely given for our instruction. From the initial chapter of this personal letter, we can see, among other things, some of the privileges, responsibilities, and opportunities that are ours as Christ's disciples. By God's grace, we have been granted life in Christ and have been gifted with the Holy Spirit. Regardless of our occupation, our Christian vocation is to live lives faithful to and unashamed of the gospel, a treasure more precious than silver or gold and more valuable than life itself.

> *. . . He would be guided and directed through the Holy Spirit who dwelt in him and in all who have entrusted their lives to Christ.*

Laying On of Hands

Have you ever attended an ordination or commissioning service in your church where people pray over and lay their hands on those who are being ordained or commissioned? If so, did you wonder about the origin and significance of such actions?

Today's lesson correlates Timothy's reception of divine endowment for ministry with Paul's laying his hands on him (2 Tim. 1:6; see also 1 Tim. 4:14; 5:22). Similarly, in Acts 6:6 the apostles prayed and laid hands on seven Greek-speaking Jews, who were set apart to distribute food to Hellenistic widows. Also, the church at Antioch prayed and laid hands on Barnabas and Saul prior to sending them off to minister (Acts 13:3).

This New Testament practice appears to have originated in Jewish circles. The clearest connection to this custom in the Old Testament is the occasion when Moses commissioned Joshua as his successor by laying his hands on him (Numbers 27:23; see Deuteronomy 34:9).

Timothy's Parents

In the passage, we discover the names of Timothy's grandmother and mother—Lois and Eunice respectively (2 Tim. 1:5). Paul described both of them as women of faith. Acts 16:1 also depicts Timothy's mother as a believer. On the other hand, his father is simply referred to as a "Greek" and is seemingly not a follower of Christ (Acts 16:1, 3).

Interestingly, Timothy's parents did not have him circumcised according to Jewish custom (see Acts 16:3). Timothy's uncircumcision was a severe breach of the Jewish faith tradition and thus illustrates one reason

Jewish people past and present are wary of marrying Gentiles. In the past, Baptist Christians have been leery of marrying non-Christians and even believers of other Christian denominations. Is this presently the case in your experience? If not, should it be? Why or why not?

Questions

1. If 2 Timothy were written by someone other than Paul, would this deeply disturb you or unsettle your faith? Why, or why not?

2. Paul referred to Timothy as his "beloved child" (2 Tim. 1:2). Do you have a "parent" in the faith? Have you been a "parent" to others in coming to and living out their Christian faith?

3. Paul maintained that he served God with a "clear conscience." How can we do the same?

4. Paul noted that Timothy's spiritual family tree included both his grandmother and mother. Do you have relatives who were integral in leading you to faith in Christ and/or in modeling the Christian life for you?

5. Paul presumed that Christians will suffer for the gospel. Do you think that the majority of contemporary American Christians suffer much, if any, for their commitment to Christ? If so, how? If not, why not?

6. How can we best balance proper belief and proper behavior?

Main Idea

Our lives will be more meaningful to ourselves and others as we single-mindedly focus on serving Christ.

Question to Explore

On what is your life focused? Or is it?

LESSON EIGHT

Living with Single-Minded Purpose

Study Aim

To decide on ways in which I will focus my life more definitely on Christ

Study and Action Emphases

- Affirm the Bible as our authoritative guide for life and ministry
- Share the gospel with all people
- Develop a growing, vibrant faith
- Equip people for servant leadership

Quick Read

In 2 Timothy 2, Paul offered Timothy specific instructions, along with fitting illustrations, as he called his spiritual "child" to focus his life and ministry more fully on Christ Jesus.

Before an athletic team takes the field or court, its coach often reiterates the game plan and tries to motivate the players. As Paul prepared to pass the "ministerial torch" to Timothy, he wanted to remind him about a number of things. Additionally, Paul wanted to impress on his spiritual protégé the primary focus and abiding importance of the faith. In this lesson we will examine Paul's instruction to Timothy as set forth in 2 Timothy 2. As we will see, this chapter is characterized by multiple exhortations and memorable illustrations.

2 Timothy 2:1–17a, 20–23

1You then, my child, be strong in the grace that is in Christ Jesus; **2**and what you have heard from me through many witnesses entrust to faithful people who will be able to teach others as well. **3**Share in suffering like a good soldier of Christ Jesus. **4**No one serving in the army gets entangled in everyday affairs; the soldier's aim is to please the enlisting officer. **5**And in the case of an athlete, no one is crowned without competing according to the rules. **6**It is the farmer who does the work who ought to have the first share of the crops. **7**Think over what I say, for the Lord will give you understanding in all things.

8Remember Jesus Christ, raised from the dead, a descendant of David—that is my gospel, **9**for which I suffer hardship, even to the point of being chained like a criminal. But the word of God is not chained. **10**Therefore

I endure everything for the sake of the elect, so that they may also obtain the salvation that is in Christ Jesus, with eternal glory. **11**The saying is sure:

If we have died with him, we will also live with him;

12if we endure, we will also reign with him;

if we deny him, he will also deny us;

13if we are faithless, he remains faithful—

for he cannot deny himself.

14Remind them of this, and warn them before God that they are to avoid wrangling over words, which does no good but only ruins those who are listening. **15**Do your best to present yourself to God as one approved by him, a worker who has no need to be ashamed, rightly explaining the word of truth. **16**Avoid profane chatter, for it will lead people into more and more impiety, **17**and their talk will spread like gangrene. . . .

● ● ● ● ● ● ● ● ● ● ● ● ● ● ● ● ●

20In a large house there are utensils not only of gold and silver but also of wood and clay, some for special use, some for ordinary. **21**All who cleanse themselves of the things I have mentioned will become special utensils, dedicated and useful to the owner of the house, ready for every good work. **22**Shun youthful passions and pursue righteousness, faith, love, and peace, along with those who call on the Lord from a pure heart. **23**Have nothing to do with stupid and senseless controversies; you know that they breed quarrels.

Be Strong in Christ Jesus (2:1–7)

At the conclusion of chapter 1, Paul informed Timothy that a certain Onesiphorus, in contrast to Phygelus and Hermogenes, had been supportive of and helpful to him, not only in Ephesus but also in Rome. Furthermore, Paul wished for Onesiphorus grace from the Lord on the Day of the Lord, that is, at the time of Christ's coming (2 Timothy 1:15–18).

As Paul approached the end of his life and ministry, he recognized that the integrity and growth of the gospel depended greatly on those who would come behind him.

Onesiphorus had demonstrated a strength and steadfastness of commitment. Paul called Timothy similarly to "be strong in the grace that is in Christ Jesus" (2 Tim. 2:1). The unmerited mercy of Christ enables faithful living for Christ. Grace typifies and undergirds the Christian life from start to finish. As the third stanza of "Amazing Grace" reminds us: "'Tis grace hath bro't [us] safe thus far, And grace will lead [us] home."[1]

Not only did Paul enjoin Timothy to be trustworthy, he also instructed him to "entrust to faithful people" that which he had heard from Paul in the presence of others so that they could teach others (2:2). As Paul approached the end of his life and ministry, he recognized that the integrity and growth of the gospel depended greatly on those who would come behind him. Paul did not regard the gospel as his own special preserve. On the contrary, he sought to share the good news with others. In turn, he hoped that people would accept and mature in the faith so that they might also teach the faith to others by word and by deed.

Having instructed Timothy to be strong in Christ and to entrust the teaching he had received to faithful people (2:1–2), Paul told Timothy for a second time to share in the suffering associated with and resulting from the gospel (2:3; see 1:8). In doing so, Timothy would be "like a good soldier of Christ Jesus." Expanding on the soldier analogy, Paul reminded Timothy that those who serve well as soldiers do not allow themselves to become entangled in comparatively trivial affairs. Rather, their ambition is to please those who enlisted them into military service (2:4). It is not difficult to discern the primary reason that Paul employed this illustration here. Even as soldiers are to take pains to honor those who enlisted them by avoiding distractions, so also believers are to focus their attention and affections on the One who signed them up for the "heavenly army."

. . . He hoped that people would accept and mature in the faith so that they might also teach the faith to others by word and by deed.

Introducing another metaphor to instruct Timothy, Paul noted that an athlete is not "crowned without competing according to the rules" (2:5). In Paul's day, winning runners would often receive a crown for their

victory (see 1 Corinthians 9:25). Here, Paul emphasized that those who would receive a prize must comply
with the rules of the game. So,
by appealing to the illustration of a soldier, Paul wanted to
stress the importance of focusing on and deferring to Christ.
Then Paul used the image of
the athlete in 2 Timothy 2:5 to
underscore the necessity of living
life according to stipulated spiritual guidelines. The
earliest followers of Jesus learned "the rules" primarily through apostolic instruction and example. Later
generations of Christians have been able to turn to the
Bible for such vital counsel.

. . . Believers are to focus their attention and affections on the One who signed them up for the "heavenly army."

In 2:6 Paul offered Timothy still another picture—
that of a hard-working farmer. Paul told Timothy that
the toiling farmer ought to have the first share of the
crops. Elsewhere, Paul employed farming imagery
to establish the point that "those who proclaim the
gospel should get their living by the gospel" (1 Corinthians 9:7; note 9:11, 14; see also 1 Tim. 5:17–18).
The primary point here, however, appears to be one of
industry. As Timothy carried out his ministry, he was
to labor like a farmer, sowing the seeds of the gospel
and reaping spiritual fruit.

Paul never explicitly explained to Timothy precisely what he had in mind by likening him to a
soldier, an athlete, and a farmer. Rather, like a good
teacher, he told Timothy to ponder further what he

was saying to him. As Timothy employed his God-given critical faculties, Paul assured him that the Lord would provide increasing clarity (2 Tim. 2:6; see Proverbs 2:6).

Remember Jesus Christ (2:8–13)

Paul had enjoined Timothy in 2:7 to think about his instruction. Now Paul offered yet another admonition in 2:8. He called Timothy to be perpetually mindful of Jesus Christ— the primary focus of his faith and the central ground of the gospel. At this point, Paul set forth a summary of the gospel that Paul preached (and Timothy embraced). Specifically mentioned is Jesus' resurrection from the dead and Jesus' Davidic ancestry. Although Paul's letters place much emphasis on Christ's resurrection (see especially 1 Cor.15), Paul did not tend to highlight the Lord's royal descent. This is understandable, given that Pauline congregations were seemingly comprised primarily of Gentiles. In writing to the Romans, however, Paul highlighted in his introductory remarks the same two facets of the gospel message referred to here (Romans 1:3–4).

. . . Paul used the image of the athlete in 2 Timothy 2:5 to underscore the necessity of living life according to stipulated spiritual guidelines.

Paul not only shared the gospel with others, but he also suffered hardship for the gospel on behalf of others (2 Tim. 2:9). Indeed, Paul was placed in chains like a criminal for the gospel. Even so, the Apostle maintained that "the word of God is not chained" (2:9). This cryptic comment could refer to Paul's ability to preach freely despite his captivity (see Acts 28:30–31; Philippians 1:7, 12–14). Paul might also be referring in this verse to his conviction that the gospel is an uncontainable force and is far more powerful and influential than any one individual, even an apostle.

As Timothy carried out his ministry, he was to labor like a farmer, sowing the seeds of the gospel and reaping spiritual fruit.

Due to the fact that the gospel continued to grow and bear fruit (see Colossians 1:6), Paul was able on behalf of "the elect" (that is, Christians) to endure various hardships (2 Tim. 2:10). Paul's suffering on behalf of the gospel enabled people to find eternal life and salvation in the person of Jesus Christ (2:10).

Verses 11–13 are hymnic in nature. Note that both verse 8 and verses 11–13 have Christ as their subject. Verse 11 begins with the statement, "The saying is sure." Three such sayings appear in 1 Timothy (1:15; 3:1; 4:9) and one in Titus (3:8). This statement in 2 Timothy is the fullest of the five. It is comprised of four conditional sentences.

The "saying" begins by maintaining that if we (that is, believers) died with Christ, as symbolized in baptism, then we will live with him at the time of the resurrection (see 2:11; see also Romans 6:3–8; Col. 2:12). The statement continues by affirming that if we "endure" ("endure" the suffering that marks life in Christ; note especially 2 Tim. 2:10; 4:5), then we will in due time reign with Christ in glory (2:12a; see again 2:10).

These first two confessions stand in stark contradiction to the claims being made by Hymenaeus and Philetus (see 2:17–18). They were claiming that the resurrection had already occurred. By doing so, they were "upsetting the faith of some" (2:18). The first two "sure" sayings, then, function to counter such claims and to reinforce the gospel that Paul preached.

The third line of this "faithful saying" declares that "if we deny him, he will also deny us" (2:12b). What might constitute denial of Christ? Is it verbal (see Matthew 10:33)? Is it ethical (see Titus 1:16)? Is it irrevocable? (Consider the cases of Judas Iscariot and Simon Peter.) The answers are uncertain, but what is not in question is the importance of fidelity in the Christian life (recall 2 Tim. 2:2). Even if our faith fluctuates, however, Christ's character is constant (2:13). He does not vacillate; rather, "Jesus Christ is the same yesterday and today and forever" (Hebrews 13:8).

Watch Your Words (2:14–17a)

At the outset of verse 14, Paul told Timothy to remind faithful people of the preceding sayings. Simultaneously, he instructed Timothy to warn believers not to wrangle over words. These admonitions appear to have been occasioned by an ongoing theological controversy that apparently had to do with the meaning of Christ's resurrection and the timing of Christians' resurrection. Paul stated that resurrection is a future hope (note 2 Tim. 2:11, 17–18).

Paul was concerned that Timothy not be swept up in and carried along by such controversy. Additionally, Paul told Timothy to "avoid profane chatter" because it would generate godlessness and grow like gangrene (2:17). On the contrary, the Apostle instructed him to strive to present himself to God as tried and true and not ashamed (2:15; see 1:8, 12). He was to "rightly" handle or explain (literally: *cut a path for*) "the word of truth" (that is, the gospel). Verses 24–25 enumerate additional qualities that are to characterize a servant of the Lord, namely, kindness, teaching ability, forbearance, and gentleness.

Be a Noble, Pure Vessel (2:20–23)

The biblical instruction set forth in 2:19 is followed by yet another illustration. This time the Apostle referred to valuable household vessels made of gold and silver on the one hand and less valuable household vessels comprised of wood and earthenware on the other hand (2:20). Although less valuable vessels might pale in price and appearance, they might still serve a valuable function for the master (2:21). Like such vessels, people who purify themselves before a holy God may be used by God for good work (see 3:17).

Even as Jesus stands at the center of this chapter of Scripture, Jesus should also be front and center in our lives.

Paul continued by exhorting Timothy to flee "youthful passions," which would include sexual sins (2:22a). The story of Joseph and Potiphar's wife serves as a positive illustration of this admonition (Genesis 39:1–23), even as the saga of Samson and Delilah affords a negative example (Judges 16:1–22). Positively, Paul enjoined Timothy to pursue "righteousness, faith [meaning *faithfulness*], love, and peace, along with those who call on the Lord from a pure heart" (2 Tim. 2:22b). Doctrinal purity should not be divorced from ethical purity lest impurity result. Jesus declared a blessing on the pure in heart. They, Jesus said, will behold God in the beauty of holiness (Matthew 5:8).

Focus On This

This lesson, although full of admonitions to and illustrations for Timothy, focuses on Jesus. Timothy was

143

to "be strong in the grace that is in *Christ Jesus*" (2:1), is to suffer "as a good soldier of *Christ Jesus*" (2:3), and is to "remember *Jesus Christ*" (2:8). Paul also spoke in 2:10 of the "salvation in *Christ Jesus*," who also serves as the primary subject of the "faithful saying" recorded in 2:11–13 (italics for emphasis).

Even as Jesus stands at the center of this chapter of Scripture, Jesus should also be front and center in our lives. Perhaps this statement strikes you as true but trite. Still, in a day when so much (and perhaps so many) clamor for our time and attention, we would do well to hear and to heed Paul's instruction to Timothy about Jesus. We would also do well to embrace similar counsel from another epistle that mentions Timothy (Hebrews 13:23). The particular passage I have in mind is Hebrews 12:2, where believers are called to look to Jesus, "the pioneer and perfecter of our faith."

The Elect

Although some theologians regard the elect as those select people that God has predestined for salvation, Paul does not appear to use this idea in such a manner. On the contrary, Paul seems to view the elect as those individuals who have responded positively to the gospel, as 2 Timothy 2:10 strongly suggests.

Prior to his conversion, Paul would have viewed faithful Israelites as the elect of God. After Paul became a follower of Jesus and a minister to the Gentiles, however, he used the term (and the related word "chosen") with respect to believers in Christ. The spiritual privileges and prerogatives that were once Israel's alone, Paul maintained were now extended to Gentiles as well. In Romans 3:29 Paul asked whether God is the God of the Jews alone. Paul answered *no* and contended that God is God of the Gentiles also. (See also the following Pauline texts related to this topic: Romans 8:33; 11:5; 16:13; Colossians 3:12; 1 Thessalonians 1:4; Titus 1:1. See also 1 Peter 2:9; 5:13.)

Descended from David

The Davidic descent of Jesus Christ is mentioned twice in Paul's letters (Rom. 1:3; 2 Tim. 2:8). Interestingly, Jesus' Davidic ancestry features far more prominently in the Gospels of Matthew and Luke. Time and again in these two Gospels Jesus is referred to and lauded as the "son of David." It appears that the connection between David and Jesus was of greater importance to Jewish Christians than to Gentile believers. Is the confession that Jesus descended from David still significant for contemporary Christians? Why or why not?

Questions

1. Paul implored Timothy to "be strong" in the Lord (2 Tim. 2:1). What helps us to "be strong in the Lord and in the strength of his power" (Ephesians 6:10)? What hinders us?

2. In 2 Timothy 2:8 Paul mentioned the resurrection and the Davidic descent of Jesus as part and parcel of the gospel he preached. What do you see other foundational features of the gospel to be?

3. Second Timothy 2:12b reads, "If we deny him, he also will deny us." How do you interpret this statement in light of the belief about "once saved, always saved"?

4. Paul encouraged Timothy to "avoid wrangling over words" (2 Tim. 2:14). How might this counsel apply in your congregational and denominational context?

NOTES

1. Words, John Newton.

Focal Text

2 Timothy
3:1–5, 10–17

Background

2 Timothy 3

Main Idea

When facing challenges to faith, take courage from the examples of faithful Christians and continue in what you have learned from the Scriptures.

Question to Explore

What resources do we have in facing challenges to our faith?

LESSON NINE Facing Challenges to Faith

Study Aim

To identify helpful ways for facing challenges to my faith

Study and Action Emphases

- Affirm the Bible as our authoritative guide for life and ministry
- Develop a growing, vibrant faith
- Equip people for servant leadership

Quick Read

As Paul continued to instruct Timothy regarding Christian life and ministry, he specified vices to avoid and virtues to cultivate.

Christians have always faced challenging times. Paul knew Timothy would face them, and he provided instructions to help him.

Paul turned at the outset of chapter 3 to remind Timothy that "in the last days distressing times" would come (2 Timothy 3:1; see also 4:3; 1 Timothy 4:1). In verse 2 of chapter 3, Paul began to instruct his junior colleague about the kinds of people he should avoid. He moved from there to instruct him to continue to practice the Christian instructions he had received and to recall the way that the faith had been lived out before him.

2 Timothy 3:1–5, 10–17

1You must understand this, that in the last days distressing times will come. **2**For people will be lovers of themselves, lovers of money, boasters, arrogant, abusive, disobedient to their parents, ungrateful, unholy, **3**inhuman, implacable, slanderers, profligates, brutes, haters of good, **4**treacherous, reckless, swollen with conceit, lovers of pleasure rather than lovers of God, **5**holding to the outward form of godliness but denying its power. Avoid them!

• • • • • • • • • • • • • • • • •

10Now you have observed my teaching, my conduct, my aim in life, my faith, my patience, my love, my steadfastness, **11**my persecutions, and my suffering the things that happened to me in Antioch, Iconium, and Lystra. What persecutions I endured! Yet the Lord rescued me from all of them. **12**Indeed, all who want to live a godly life in Christ Jesus will be persecuted. **13**But wicked people and impostors will go from bad to worse, deceiving others and being deceived. **14**But as for you, continue in what you have learned and firmly believed, knowing from whom you learned it, **15**and how from childhood you have known the sacred writings that are able to instruct you for salvation through faith in Christ Jesus. **16**All scripture is inspired by God and is useful for teaching, for reproof, for correction, and for training in righteousness, **17**so that everyone who belongs to God may be proficient, equipped for every good work.

The Evil Ways of the Last Days (3:1–5)

In verses 2–5 Paul listed various vices that are to typify people in the "last days." Before considering this catalog, however, let us pause to examine the expression "last days." Understandably, we tend to think about this phrase with special reference to ourselves and to our present experiences in this world. Any given generation could well be the last one, and the end of time could come sooner than later.

Many early Christians seem to have thought they were living in the last days. If we were to ask why, our answer would need to take into account the common conviction among the earliest believers that Jesus' life, death, and resurrection coupled with God's sending of the Holy Spirit inaugurated the beginning of the end (note, for example, Acts 2:17; Romans 13:11; 1 Corinthians 7:29; 10:11). That being the case, they maintained that the next cosmic event of God's work as revealed in Christ was to be Christ's Second Coming. It is in that sense those who first followed Jesus believed they were living in the last days and anticipated the culmination of human history through Jesus Christ in the not too distant future. As in our day, some early believers appear to have had a more acute sense of Christ's imminent return than others (note 2 Thessalonians 2:1–2; see Revelation 1:1; 22:6, 10).

Even as Jesus was subject to persecution, Jesus' genuine followers should come to grips with the very real possibility that their lives might also be marked by such hostility.

Many early Christians expected the time preceding the end to be marked by precipitous moral decline. In 2 Timothy 3:2–4, no less than eighteen vices are cataloged as indicating this anticipated behavioral breakdown. (For other vice lists in Paul's letters, see Romans 1:29–31; 1 Corinthians 5:11; 6:9–10; 2 Corinthians 12:20; Galatians 5:19–21; and Colossians 3:6, 8). Paul in 2 Timothy 3:2–4 stated that in the tumultuous times marking the end, instead of loving God, people will love themselves, money, and pleasure. Moreover, they will be proud, arrogant, and swollen with conceit. Hating the good, they will be "abusive, disobedient to their parents, ungrateful, unholy, inhuman, implacable, slanderers, profligates, brutes, haters of good, treacherous," and "reckless." To top it all off, such people will hold to a form of piety but deny its transformative power. A religion that does not inform and empower a person for moral action is here declared to be a spiritual charade that is impotent and empty (2 Tim. 3:5).

Taken together, verses 2–5a don't present a pretty picture! Neither are they intended to. Paul's purpose here was to dissuade Timothy from being derailed by such people. This explains Paul's admonition to his younger coworker in 3:5b to "avoid" those who possess and espouse a false piety, an empty spirituality. This passage does not set forth a precise timetable for the advent of such moral waywardness, and its description of godless people is both general and repetitive. However, the fact that opponents were present who posed a real threat to the spiritual stability of some believers gives this text a ring of authenticity as well as a degree of urgency. (Compare 1 John 2:18, which speaks of the "last hour" on the one hand and specific opponents [the "many antichrists"] on the other.)

> *Our own spiritual health will be enhanced if we will recall those who have led us to, and built us up in, our faith.*

Specifically, Paul mentioned male teachers who were preying on vulnerable female learners (2 Tim. 3:6).

The depiction of these particular women is far from flattering ("weak women" overwhelmed by sins and swayed by sundry desires, who were instructed perpetually but fruitlessly, 3:6–7). The "false teachers," though, drew an even shorter stick. They were not only likened to the two Egyptian magicians who opposed Moses (see Exodus 7:11–12, 22; 8:7), but they are also said to be corrupt in mind, counterfeit in faith, and opposed to the truth (2 Tim. 3:8). Appearances notwithstanding, Paul said that these teachers would not win the day. On the contrary, Paul contended that as with Jannes and Jambres, the names given these two magicians in Jewish tradition, their folly would become clear to everybody (3:9).

> . . . The Scriptures were for Paul a spiritual resource into which he and other believers might tap and to which they might turn time and again.

An Example to Embrace (3:10–13)

Having admonished Timothy to avoid those people who laid claim on the faith but lacked moral compass and doctrinal moorings, Paul reminded his protégé of the way he, Timothy, had learned Christ. For starters, Timothy was privy to Paul's instruction in the faith. Additionally, Timothy had witnessed first hand the way that the Apostle lived out the gospel he proclaimed. Timothy had the opportunity to witness that Paul practiced what he professed. Timothy also observed up close and personal Paul's singular purpose in life—his "aim in life" (3:10)—to pursue and please Christ (note also 2 Cor. 5:9; Philippians 3:13–14).

Other virtues that Timothy saw in Paul included the Apostle's fidelity, tenacity, and charity (2 Tim. 3:10). Furthermore, Timothy knew first hand various persecutions and sufferings that had befallen Paul as he carried out his ministry. Paul specifically mentioned in 3:11 the persecution that he endured at Pisidian Antioch, Iconium, and Lystra. According to Acts 13—14, during the course of Paul's so-called first missionary journey, he was opposed in each of these cities (see Acts 13:50; 14:5–6, 19–20).

Christians have always faced challenging times.

The persecution was particularly acute in Lystra, the town where Timothy lived (16:1). In Lystra, opponents stoned Paul, dragged him outside the city, and left him for dead (see 2 Cor. 11:25). Paul testified that the Lord rescued him from each of these perilous situations.

Such troubles were not limited to apostles, though. Paul declared that "all those who want to live a godly life in Christ Jesus will be persecuted" (2 Tim. 3:12). Personal experience and theological beliefs led Paul to anticipate and to accept suffering as part and parcel of the faith. Paul told Timothy to expect and embrace this stark reality. Even as Jesus was subject to persecution, Jesus' genuine followers should come to grips with the very real possibility that their lives might also be marked by such hostility.

The suffering of believers aspiring to godliness to which Paul subscribed in principle was due in no small part to his own experience with unprincipled people. Those whom Paul depicted as morally evil people and masqueraders of the faith would, he maintained in 3:13, descend further still, going "from bad to worse." Not only would they lead people astray, but they themselves would also be deceived.

The unavoidable, if uncomfortable, implication of verses 12–13 is that Christ-followers should not think for even a fleeting moment that discipleship will be constituted entirely of sweetness and light. Darkest night must be endured. Fresh drink and light will come on the Day of days. However, while it is still called *today*, Christians along with creation and the Spirit groan for redemption, God's setting aright through Christ a world gone awry (see especially Rom. 8:18–30).

Enfleshed and Inscribed Texts (3:14–17)

That being said, Paul charged Timothy not to give way to doubt or despair. Rather, Paul told Timothy to continue to abide in the faith that he had received and believed. In doing so, Timothy was to recall the people from whom he had learned the faith. This would include Paul, his father in the faith; Lois, his grandmother; and Eunice, his mother (see 2 Tim. 1:5). It would also have involved a network of others who are lesser known or unknown to us. Not a few people would have taught Timothy in the faith and would have modeled the faith for Timothy.

Our own spiritual health will be enhanced if we will recall those who have led us to, and built us up in, our faith. It is equally important for us to reach out to others in our spheres of influence who are in need of the message and model of the gospel.

Not only was Timothy the beneficiary of good and godly models in the faith, but he was also from childhood made knowledge-able of the "sacred writings." The sacred writ of which 3:15 speaks is almost certainly the same as the "scripture" referred to in 3:16. Timothy's knowledge of such writings was spiritually advantageous. They "are able to instruct you for salvation through faith in Christ Jesus."

When we are steeped in and steered by the Scriptures, then our spiritual lives will be marked by maturity.

Interestingly, the expressed aim of the "sacred writings" in 3:15 is that they are able to impart wisdom, which in turn directs one to salvation. Equally fascinating is the idea that these "sacred writings" are able to position one for salvation "through faith in Christ Jesus." Elsewhere in Paul we encounter the conviction that the Scriptures, even though written in earlier days to Israel, were "written for our [that is, "Christian"] instruction" (Rom. 15:4), "upon whom the end of the ages has come" (1 Cor. 10:11, author's translation). Far from being a mere collection of ancient documents, then, the Scriptures were for Paul a spiritual resource into which he and other believers might tap and to which they might turn time and again.

If one were to ask why Paul so deeply appreciated and readily appropriated the Scriptures, one could find at least a partial answer in 2 Timothy 3:16. There one encounters the well-known remark, "All scripture is inspired by God." Paul did not enumerate the particular writings to which he referred as Scripture (see 2 Peter 1:20). Likely, though, those books of which he spoke here would not differ greatly from what we now call the Old Testament. Over time as the documents that presently comprise our New Testament were composed, circulated, and collected, the church also came to view them as "inspired." The God who hovered over the waters, breathed life into Adam, and anointed Jesus as God's Son (see Genesis 1:1–2; 2:7; Luke 4:18) also animated the Scriptures by his Spirit.

According to 2 Timothy 3:16, Scripture is both inspired by God and profitable for people.

According to 2 Timothy 3:16, Scripture is both inspired by God and profitable for people. Although not every section of Scripture may be riveting or readily applicable to one's particular life circumstances, it can still be seen as profitable. Verse 16 specifies four ways that Scripture is useful: it teaches; it reproves or rebukes; corrects; and trains in righteousness. Scripture functions positively and negatively in our lives. That is, it builds us up and breaks us down; it comforts us in affliction and afflicts us in comfort. It speaks and shapes, delights and disturbs. It gives us a vision of God and the good, and it guides, and at points goads, us, to embrace this vision, to become people marked by righteousness.

When we are steeped in and steered by the Scriptures, then our spiritual lives will be marked by maturity. We will avoid the kinds of vices enumerated in 3:2–4 and will cultivate the virtues set forth in 3:10–11. Additionally, we will be able to discern more clearly and fully who and what we should and should not listen to and live for. In brief, Scripture encourages our spiritual formation and prepares us to be agents of transformation, equipped for and engaged in "every good work" in and outside the church. The fact that our study of and reflection on Scripture readies us for service should be motivation enough for us all to dig deeper into and linger longer over what we have come to regard as "wonderful words of life."[1]

Paul's (Dis)regard for Women

It is not uncommon for Paul to be viewed as a male chauvinist. Passages from the pastoral epistles tend to give rise and even substance to this widespread impression (see especially 1 Timothy 2:8–15; 5:14; 2 Timothy 3:6–7; Titus 2:3–5).

To be sure, Paul was not a twenty-first century person conscious of and committed to contemporary notions of egalitarianism. That being said, it is important to keep at least two things in mind when reading Paul's remarks about women and wives: (1) He did not make these statements in a vacuum. They were occasioned by and directed to particular concerns in specific settings. To be sure, this does not necessarily explain away *what* he says, but it does help us to understand more fully *why* he said it. (2) Additionally and importantly, Paul did minister alongside women in carrying out his mission, including but not limited to the following: Phoebe, a deacon (Rom. 16:1; see 1 Tim. 3:11); Prisca, a co-worker and host of Pauline congregations (Rom. 16:3–5; 1 Cor. 16:19); Junia, noteworthy among the apostles (Rom. 16:7); Euodia and Syntyche, co-workers in Philippi (Phil. 4:2–3); and Lydia and Nympha, hosts of Pauline assemblies in their homes (Acts 16:14–15, 40; Colossians 4:15). So, before being too harsh on the Apostle Paul on his views on women, these facts should be considered also.

Formation of the New Testament Canon

If the New Testament did not float down from heaven on golden plates, then how did we get it? To put the matter simply, it happened gradually and informally. As documents were composed and circulated, Christians formed various collections. As early as the middle of the second century, Marcion had formed a canon composed of a number of Paul's letters as well as most of the Gospel of Luke. The earliest list of the twenty-seven documents present in our New Testament is dated to A.D. 367, when Athanasius, bishop of Alexandria, enumerated these works in a letter he wrote to people under his pastoral care and oversight.

Questions

1. How do you feel about the thought that Christians have been living in what may be described as "the last days" for some 2,000 years now?

2. In what ways do we contemporary Christians hold to a form of religion while denying its power?

3. What is the nature and purpose of Scripture according to 2 Timothy 3:15–17?

4. What do the Scriptures mean to you, and how would you describe your relationship to the Bible?

NOTES

1. Hymn, "Wonderful Words of Life," words and music by Philip P. Bliss.

Main Idea

The legacies people leave and from which we learn can enhance our Christian life and ministry.

Question to Explore

What sort of legacy are you leaving? following?

LESSON
TEN

Leaving—and Learning from—a Legacy

Study Aim

To describe legacies from which I have benefited and summarize the legacy I wish to leave to others

Study and Action Emphases

- Affirm the Bible as our authoritative guide for life and ministry
- Share the gospel with all people
- Develop a growing, vibrant faith
- Encourage healthy families
- Equip people for servant leadership

Quick Read

Paul offered final instructions to his ministerial colleague, even as he anticipated and contemplated the conclusion of his own life and ministry.

People are not ready to live until they are ready to die, it is said. It has also been stated that those who die well have lived well (and vice versa).

These adages seem appropriate to Paul the Apostle. On the one hand, Paul was acutely aware of his frailty and mortality. He recognized and embraced the transitory nature of human existence. After his conversion, he was committed to giving himself wholly to Christ whether in life or in death (see 2 Corinthians 4:16—5:10). That is illustrated by his now familiar words to the Philippians: "For to me to live is Christ and to die is gain" (Philippians 1:21, author's translation). On the other hand, as Paul stood on the precipice of death, which he apparently did when writing 2 Timothy, he was able to do so with the complete confidence that his earthly departure would be met with heavenly reward (2 Timothy 4:6–8).

Among other things, this lesson affords us the opportunity to reflect on our commitments and to contemplate what looking at our lives in a "rear view mirror" might reveal. If in the final analysis our investments in the cause of Christ are the only ones that endure, how affluent are our spiritual portfolios? Are we making a difference as well as a living? Are we resting on our spiritual laurels? Have we retired spiritually as well as professionally? The text before us, particularly 4:6–8, causes us to ask and calls us to answer questions of import for both the here and the hereafter.

2 Timothy 4:1–8

¹In the presence of God and of Christ Jesus, who is to judge the living and the dead, and in view of his appearing and his kingdom, I solemnly urge you: ²proclaim the message; be persistent whether the time is favorable or unfavorable; convince, rebuke, and encourage, with the utmost patience in teaching. ³For the time is coming when people will not put up with sound doctrine, but having itching ears, they will accumulate for themselves teachers to suit their own desires, ⁴and will turn away from listening to the truth and wander away to myths. ⁵As for you, always be sober, endure suffering, do the work of an evangelist, carry out your ministry fully.

⁶As for me, I am already being poured out as a libation, and the time of my departure has come. ⁷I have fought the good fight, I have finished the race, I have kept the faith. ⁸From now on there is reserved for me the crown of righteousness, which the Lord, the righteous judge, will give me on that day, and not only to me but also to all who have longed for his appearing.

Paul's Final Charge to Timothy (4:1–5)

Paul had stated what Scripture is—inspired and profitable—and had briefly elaborated on how Scripture can help to shape a person for "every good work" (1 Tim. 3:16–17). Now Paul proceeded in chapter 4 to offer Timothy additional ministerial counsel. At the outset of the chapter, the Apostle issued his spiritual successor a series of sober and solemn charges (4:1–5). The fact that Paul offered such instruction "before God and Christ Jesus" adds gravity to these injunctions, not to mention an increased sense of sanctity and accountability (4:1, author's translation; see 1 Tim. 5:21).

Paul further reinforced his instruction in 2 Timothy 4:2 by appealing in 4:1 to Christ's "appearing and his kingdom." (The word translated "appearing" gives us our word *epiphany*.) Additionally, Christ is depicted in 4:1 as "the one who is about to judge the living and the dead" (author's translation). It is as if Paul, an apostolic attorney, was placing Timothy, a pivotal witness, before the divine judgment bar so as to impress on him the eternal importance of what he was about to say.

If in the final analysis our investments in the cause of Christ are the only ones that endure, how affluent are our spiritual portfolios?

Verse 2 contains five staccato-styled admonitions. To begin, Paul enjoined Timothy to "preach the word" (author's translation). Paul did not elaborate on the "word" he told Timothy to proclaim. The likely reference, though, is to the gospel (see also 2 Tim. 2:15). The focus of this preached word is none other than Jesus Christ himself. The contents of this proclamation would include the declaration that Jesus, who was by virtue of his incarnation a descendant of David, was by means of his resurrection the living and coming Lord (see 2:8–9).

Paul also called Timothy to be "persistent in season and out of season" (4:2, author's translation). For the Christian in general and the Christian minister in particular, there is no such thing as a spiritual vacation. I remember a question I once asked my mother during the summer following my first grade year. Seeing that we had a lengthy break from school, I inquired as to whether we could also enjoy an extended break from church. Much to my chagrin at the time, I was informed that there was no such thing as a spiritual break. Paul impressed on Timothy the urgency and necessity of ministry at all times, be they good or bad. Being a Christian is a *24/7* proposition, an eternal vocation. An urgent message requires a diligent, vigilant response from its messengers. So it is with the gospel and those who bear it.

Are we making a difference as well as a living?

Paul continued his instruction of Timothy by enjoining him to "convince, admonish, and encourage" those entrusted to his spiritual care (4:2, author's translation). Those who minister to others must not only discern what to say, but they must also know when and how best to speak. At times people need spiritual persuasion. At other times they require exhortation. Still on other occasions words of affirmation or consolation are in order. Sometimes a spiritual pat on the back is in order. Occasionally, a spiritual swift kick in the seat may be necessary. There is no *one-size-fits-all* or *connect-the-dots* approach to ministry. Timothy was to learn with increasing skill and insight how to "speak the truth in love" (Ephesians 4:15).

What is more, Paul enjoined Timothy to conduct his ministry "with all patience and teaching" (2 Tim. 4:2, author's translation). It is all too easy to grow weary in well-doing. Those who minister are to be marked by patience. Patience is a fruit of the Spirit as well as a divine attribute. Furthermore, instruction is an integral part of ministry. Intentional, responsible teaching can inform and inspire, guide and guard, challenge and affirm. Faithful ministers, then, are patient teachers who themselves are learning patience.

Paul impressed on Timothy the urgency and necessity of ministry at all times. . . .

Paul underscored the importance of patient, spiritual instruction in 4:3. There he indicated that there will be a time, perhaps sooner than later (see 3:1–9), when people will not "put up with sound" teaching. On the contrary, the Apostle contended, they will seek out teachers who will say what they want to hear. In so doing, Paul pessimistically but realistically predicted that those with "itching ears" will stray from the truth. They will turn to "myths," mere stories that spring from a fertile imagination instead of reliable Christian tradition.

In contrast to those who stray and turn away from the truth of the gospel, Paul urged Timothy to be characterized by consistency, to be steady (2 Tim. 4:5). Vacillation in the faith is to be avoided. Fidelity is to be cultivated and embraced. As in the fable of the tortoise and the hare, steadfastness is viewed here as an essential component to completing the race.

Not only was Timothy to be steady spiritually, but he was also, Paul reiterated, to "endure suffering" (4:5; note again 1:8; 2:3). Perhaps Paul saw in Timothy a tendency to shrink back from opposition instead of standing firm in the face of affliction. Paul underscored yet again the need to be steadfast in suffering lest one's faith flag.

Additionally, Paul admonished Timothy to "do the work of an evangelist." Such labor might entail a variety of ministries but would certainly center on the proclamation of and instruction in the gospel, that is, the glad tidings announced by and effected through Jesus Christ. We tend to relegate such work to Billy Graham and a church's "hired hands." Paul, though, saw evangelism as a gift Christ entrusted to some believers (note Ephesians 4:11; see Acts 21:8) and also as a responsibility of all Christians, including Timothy.

> . . . As Paul looked back over his life he was able to say with integrity that he had run the race and fought the fight of faith with fidelity.

Last, Paul admonished Timothy in 4:5 to "fulfill [his] ministry" (author's translation). As 1 and 2 Timothy reveal, the ministry given to Timothy was multifaceted. In fact, the whole of his life and work in Christ might be collectively thought of as his ministry. Whatever else ministry was to Paul, it was foundationally *gospel* ministry. In a day when so many worthy causes compete for our attention, Christian congregations need to redouble their efforts to keep the gospel in the forefront in all they do and say.

Paul's Impending Departure from Timothy (4:6–8)

In issuing these final instructions to Timothy, Paul referred to various adversaries he had encountered (note 2 Tim. 4:10, 14, 16). Disappointments and difficulties notwithstanding, one does not find in the final lines of this letter a defeated, disillusioned Christian. Rather, as Paul anticipated his impending "departure" (that is, his approaching death), he exuded a confidence afforded by his lengthy, sacrificial obedience to the Lord.

. . . Christian congregations need to redouble their efforts to keep the gospel in the forefront in all they do and say.

That Timothy would faithfully conduct his ministry becomes all the more pressing in light of Paul's imminent passing. To speak of his soon-coming death, Paul employed sacrificial imagery. We are not, of course, to take literally Paul's statement in 4:6 that he was already being sacrificed. (Otherwise, he would hardly have been able to write to Timothy!) We are nevertheless meant to consider this statement carefully. By speaking of his death as a sacrifice, Paul was able to frame the giving of life as an act of worship (see Romans 12:1–2; Philippians 2:17).

As Paul approached his death for Christ, he reflected tersely on his life in Christ (2 Tim. 4:7). To do so, he employed athletic imagery. In retrospect the apostle declared that he had fought the "good fight" of faith. Paul had been engaged in the most significant contest of all and had not given up (see 1 Corinthians 9:24–27). The race in which he had strenuously competed he had now successfully completed (see also Phil. 3:13–14). Far from pulling up short with a hamstrung faith, the Apostle had persevered to the end and was now about to cross the finish line.

> *. . . He had the confidence of knowing that he had lived his life for the Lord.*

Based on his consistent commitment to Christ in life, Paul expected a "crown of righteousness" after death (2 Tim. 4:8). In Paul's day a crown represented a prize or reward bestowed on the victor, as with the crown given to the winners of various contests in the ancient Isthmian games. The righteousness that described and defined the spiritual crown to which Paul referred is, like the crown itself, a gift from the Lord, who is aptly depicted here as "the righteous judge."

This "crown of righteousness," like Paul's death, lay in the future. In fact, Paul joined this crowning with the "appearing" of Christ at the End (4:8; see also 1 Thessalonians 2:19; Phil. 2:17; 4:1). Until that time, Paul was willing to entrust himself to his trustworthy Lord (2 Tim. 1:12).

It was not only the Apostle, however, who was able to anticipate "the crown of righteousness." The Lord will grant the same, Paul maintains, "to all who have loved his appearing" (4:8, author's translation). Anticipation of and preparation for the Lord's appearing is an expression of one's devotion to and affection for the Lord.

A question posed by this lesson is precisely what our legacy will be.

We see inserted on gravestones a hyphen between a person's year of birth and year of death. That little punctuation mark is a testimony to life's brevity. A hyphen on a grave marker may also prompt one to wonder to whom and to what the deceased person was devoted.

By his own admission, Paul was far from being a perfect person (Phil. 3:12). In fact, he indicated a deep and abiding regret for having persecuted Christians prior to his conversion (see, for example, 1 Cor. 15:9–10; 1 Tim. 1:15–16). Nonetheless, as Paul looked back over his life he was able to say with integrity that he had run the race and fought the fight of faith with fidelity.

As Paul anticipated giving an account of his life to the Lord (note 1 Cor. 4:4–5; 2 Cor. 5:10), he had the confidence of knowing that he had lived his life for the Lord. Moreover, as Paul contemplated his departure, he was now ready to place his apostolic mantle on Timothy. As it was with Moses and Joshua and with Elijah and Elisha, so now it was to be with Paul and Timothy. The Apostle was entrusting his spiritual legacy to his dearly beloved Timothy.

What changes do you need to make so that you, like Paul, can face the future with freshness and confidence?

There is no question that we, too, will leave a legacy. A question posed by this lesson is precisely what our legacy will be. Is that for which we are living worthy of our lives? When we die, will it make an eternal difference that we lived? Since, as my father puts it, "life is not a dress rehearsal," how is your "performance" going? What changes do you need to make so that you, like Paul, can face the future with freshness and confidence?

Jesus' Appearing

In 1 Corinthians and 1 Thessalonians Paul described the Second Advent of Christ as a "coming" (Greek: *parousia*). In the pastoral epistles, though, he referred to the Lord's return as an "appearance" (author's translation; Greek, *epiphaneia*). For the use of "appearance" in this fashion in the pastorals, see 1 Timothy 6:14; 2 Timothy 4:1, 8; and Titus 2:13. (Interestingly, 2 Timothy 1:10 speaks of Jesus' initial appearance on earth as an "appearing," using the same Greek word.) These texts teach that at the time of Jesus' "appearing" or "manifestation," he will "judge the living and the dead" and will establish his eternal rule.

Paul's Death

Second Timothy 4:6 speaks of Paul's "departure," or death, as near. The New Testament, however, does not record Paul's death or reveal any of the particulars surrounding it. Church tradition reports that Paul was beheaded in Rome during the later part of the reign of the Emperor Nero, who ruled from A.D. 54–68. *First Clement*, a writing found in a collection known as the *Apostolic Fathers* and generally dated to the end of the first century A.D., may allude to Paul's martyrdom (*First Clement* 5.6–7). For the writer of *First Clement*, Paul was the prime example of one who lived and died for Christ.

Questions

1. What might lead us to gravitate toward only those teachers who say what we want to hear?

2. Who is to do the "work of an evangelist" (2 Tim. 4:5) today? How should this sacred task be approached?

3. What would you like people to be able to say about you with little exaggeration at your funeral?

4. Who has left a legacy in which you are presently living? What is the nature of this legacy?

5. Second Timothy 4:8 depicts the Lord as a "righteous judge." What is your reaction to this description?

Introducing

TITUS: *Putting Things in Order*

Reading Paul's Letter to Titus along with Paul's First and Second Letters to Timothy reveals similarities between both the people to whom the letters were written and the letters themselves. Titus was a partner of Paul in ministry, as was Timothy. Titus is identified as Paul's "loyal child in the faith" (Titus 1:4), as Timothy was (1 Timothy 1:2).[1] Paul's Letter to Titus offered Titus guidance for his ministry in a difficult place, Crete (see Titus 1:5), even as 1 and 2 Timothy offered Timothy guidance for his own ministry.

The Letter to Titus contains themes similar to those in 1 Timothy. These similar themes include instructions about: church leaders (see 1 Tim. 3; Titus 1:5–9); maintaining sound doctrine (1 Tim. 1:3; Titus 2:1); relating to government (1 Tim. 2:1–2; Titus 3:1–2); and relating to people of varying ages and roles (Titus 2:1–15; 1 Tim. 5:1—6:2a).

The Scripture passages to be studied in Titus have been selected with a view toward studying the significant texts in Titus while at the same time avoiding repetition of themes dealt with in previous lessons from the pastoral letters. Within each of the two lessons are passages that are unique to Titus in emphasis.

TITUS: PUTTING THINGS IN ORDER

Lesson 11.   Life in the Fellowship of Faith   Titus 2:1–14

Lesson 12.   Bottom-Line Christianity   Titus 3:1–9

Additional Resources for Studying Titus[2]

James D. G. Dunn. "The First and Second Letters to Timothy and the Letter to Titus." *The New Interpreter's Bible*. Volume XI. Nashville, Tennessee: Abingdon Press, 2000.

Donald Guthrie. *The Pastoral Epistles*. Revised edition. Tyndale New Testament Commentaries. Grand Rapids, Michigan: William B. Eerdmans Publishing Company, 1990.

E. Glenn Hinson. "1—2 Timothy and Titus." *The Broadman Bible Commentary*. Volume 11. Nashville, Tennessee: Broadman Press, 1971.

George W. Knight III. *Commentary on the Pastoral Epistles.* New International Greek Testament Commentary. Grand Rapids, Michigan: William B. Eerdmans Publishing Company, 1992

Thomas D. Lea and Hayne P. Griffin, Jr. *1, 2 Timothy, Titus*. The New American Commentary. Volume 34. Nashville, Tennessee: Broadman Press, 1992.

A. T. Robertson. *Word Pictures in the New Testament.*
    Volume IV. Nashville, Tennessee: Broadman Press,
    1931.

NOTES

1. Unless otherwise indicated, all Scripture quotations in this introduction and the lessons on Titus are from the New Revised Standard Version.
2. Listing a book does not imply full agreement by the writers or BAPTISTWAY PRESS® with all of its comments.

Focal Text

Titus 2:1–14

Background

Titus 2:1–15;
1 Timothy
5:1—6:2a

Main Idea

Christians are to live godly lives
in all of their life circumstances
in light of the grace of God
in Jesus Christ and the hope
Christ offers for the future.

Question to Explore

How should you live as a Christian
in the circumstances of your life?

LESSON ELEVEN

Life in the Fellowship of Faith

Study Aim

To identify ways for living as a
Christian in my life circumstances

Study and Action Emphases

- Affirm the Bible as our authoritative guide for life and ministry
- Develop a growing, vibrant faith
- Include all God's family in decision-making and service
- Value all people as created in the image of God
- Encourage healthy families

Quick Read

In contrast to the passions of the world is the gift of grace. Paul encouraged Titus and the church at Crete to embrace sound doctrine, not as a way to judge and divide but as the basis on which to emulate freely Christ's love in their lives.

Where are we? How much longer? Are we there yet? Why do we have to go anyway?

As a child, do you remember going on trips? My mother was from rural Mississippi. Every summer our family made the eternal trek on two-lane roads through rural Georgia, Alabama, and Mississippi. The scenery never changed. Rolling hills and pine trees. I thought we would never arrive.

One particular trip made a lasting impression. My older sister was sixteen and had just begun to drive. On the way home, for some reason, she decided to pass a car on a hill. As fate would have it, just as she passed the car, a semi tractor-trailer came over the crest of the hill and proceeded to descend on us like some prehistoric flying reptile. My sister had the sense to veer off to the left. The car went down an incline and came to a stop in a ditch. We were stuck, but we were safe.

Being the smart-aleck twelve-year-old that I was, I remember asking my sister something to the effect of, *Do you have any other bright ideas?* She was in shock, but far be it from me to offer any sympathy. My father, however, after making sure we were okay, patiently talked through with my sister what had happened. Never once did he chide her. How my father reacted made an indelible impression.

Sadly, I was too young at the time to realize the importance of the lesson learned in the midst of the journey. Likewise, where things religious are concerned, we often fail to see the presence of God in the midst of life, and we too readily dismiss the joy of community because we are preoccupied other things. We can even be preoccupied with a certain understanding of "sound doctrine" (Titus 2:1) rather than the grace to which it leads.

Paul wrote, "But as for you, teach what is consistent with sound doctrine" (2:1). Why such an emphasis on sound doctrine? The question is an important one to ponder, for an incorrect understanding of Paul's perspective can render doctrine nothing more than a tool of the law and its judgment. In his emphasis on sound doctrine, Paul cautioned Titus about the implications for the young and old as well as slaves. Let us begin, though, with gaining an understanding of Paul's idea of "sound doctrine."

Titus 2:1–14

¹But as for you, teach what is consistent with sound doctrine. ²Tell the older men to be temperate, serious, prudent, and sound in faith, in love, and in endurance.

³Likewise, tell the older women to be reverent in behavior, not to be slanderers or slaves to drink; they are to teach what is good, ⁴so that they may encourage the young women to love their husbands, to love their children, ⁵to be self-controlled, chaste, good managers of the household, kind, being submissive to their husbands, so that the word of God may not be discredited.

6Likewise, urge the younger men to be self-controlled. **7**Show yourself in all respects a model of good works, and in your teaching show integrity, gravity, **8**and sound speech that cannot be censured; then any opponent will be put to shame, having nothing evil to say of us.

9Tell slaves to be submissive to their masters and to give satisfaction in every respect; they are not to talk back, **10**not to pilfer, but to show complete and perfect fidelity, so that in everything they may be an ornament to the doctrine of God our Savior.

11For the grace of God has appeared, bringing salvation to all, **12**training us to renounce impiety and worldly passions, and in the present age to live lives that are self-controlled, upright, and godly, **13**while we wait for the blessed hope and the manifestation of the glory of our great God and Savior, Jesus Christ. **14**He it is who gave himself for us that he might redeem us from all iniquity and purify for himself a people of his own who are zealous for good deeds.

Sound Doctrine—the Need and a Caution (2:1)

In order to get at the heart of the text, consider Paul's intent in articulating the need for sound doctrine. For example, if one reads the text from the perspective of a legal list of things that one must do in order to be holy, the result can be a precipitous path that leads us to become too readily engrossed in the doctrine itself rather than the end to which the doctrine points. Suddenly, adherence to the doctrine becomes more important than the relationship one has through faith in Christ. Then holiness tends to mean how we compare with others and how others measure up to us rather than what God creates within us.

By focusing on sound doctrine as end in itself, one of two things results. On the one hand, some turn the sound doctrine against them- selves. They begin to believe that they don't quite measure up to all that God expects. In light of our own obvious shortcomings,

Why such an emphasis on sound doctrine?

we may start trying to figure out how we can put the blame on somebody else. In such a situation, church too easily becomes a place of judgment.

Or, if we do not let the sound doctrine burden us, we use it to justify our own sense of purity. Do you recall the parable that Jesus told in Luke's Gospel about the Pharisee and the tax collector (see Luke 18:9–14)? The Pharisee thanked God that he was, as Eugene Peterson expresses it in *The Message*, "not like other people—robbers, crooks, adulterers, or, heaven forbid, like this tax man." In the Pharisee's view, he met the letter of the law by fasting twice a week and tithing on all his income. The tax man, on the other hand, thoroughly humbled by his own sin, simply said, "God, give mercy. Forgive me, a sinner."[1] From the perspective of the Pharisee, sound doctrine was paramount because it enabled him to condemn others that he deemed not as pure or righteous as himself.

The Value of Sound Doctrine (2:1)

But why is it that Paul called Titus to focus on sound doctrine? Was it because Paul wanted people to be able to judge one another? Was it because Paul believed that adherence to sound doctrine would result in salvation? Or did Paul have some larger point in mind?

> *Suddenly, adherence to the doctrine becomes more important than the relationship one has through faith in Christ.*

An insight into Paul's thinking can be found in the opening verses of the letter that express Paul's service as being "for the sake of the faith of God's elect and the knowledge of the truth that is in accordance with godliness, in the hope of eternal life" (Titus 1:1–2). This emphasis reminds us of Paul's insistence elsewhere that the essence of what it means to be a follower of Christ is to have faith, hope, and, most importantly, love (see 1 Corinthians 13).

Paul wanted to emphasize that sound doctrine must never be regarded as an end in and of itself. Rather it always is to be seen as a bridge to the larger faith, knowledge, and hope of those who believe. Too, Paul wanted to emphasize the proper form of faith that would lead to grace. In this context, the doctrine is not the end, but rather the form or shape that leads to the mastery of the subject, which is faith in God's grace that is the truth and hope of Jesus Christ.

Why specifically was it that Paul wanted Titus to link doctrine to faith and to provide a model that the adherents at Crete could emulate? Paul had expressed his concerns to Titus in chapter 1 about the need to reject the "idle talkers and deceivers, especially those of the circumcision party" (Titus 1:9). Their being of the circumcision party highlights the fact that the church at Crete was struggling with the issue of faith in the law versus faith in Jesus Christ. In response to these "idle talkers," who emphasized circumcision as essential to belief in God, Paul admonished Titus to teach sound doctrine grounded not in the law of the Judaizers but rather in the grace of Jesus Christ.

From the perspective of the Pharisee, sound doctrine was paramount because it enabled him to condemn others that he deemed not as pure or righteous as himself.

The "idle talkers," in their preoccupation with the law, were in contrast to the "sound doctrine" that Paul wanted to emphasize. The law resulted only in condemnation and division. Likewise, theology, when it becomes an end in and of itself, can do the same. But Paul desired to convey that the "sound doctrine" that Titus was to teach and the church was to follow was not an end in itself. Rather, Paul hoped that the young church would come to see the doctrine as a bridge to the grace that only Christ's love affords. Otherwise, they—and we—would lose sight of the real end to which sound doctrine points, the joy of communion with God.

The Fruits of Sound Doctrine (2:2–14)

Recall the story about my sister's not-so-perfect drive. Dad could have burdened her with the guilt of the law had he intended to do so. Rather, though, he used the moment to embody grace and offer a word of wisdom. I think this was Paul's intent as well. Paul instructed Titus to "tell the older men to be temperate, serious, prudent, and sound in faith, in love, and in endurance" (Titus 2:2).[2] "To be temperate," or *to be sober*, sets the tone for understanding the passage. Paul's point has to do with the need to *be sober* in terms of judgment, word, and deed.

God's love is the end to which sound doctrine points.

Likewise, in 2:3–5, Paul cautioned the older women to be positive role models for younger women in order to provide stability in the home. In a society where women were regarded as property, the only hope for a young woman for an education was that received through the tutelage of older women. If the family was to be a source of stability in the Cretan society, it would in no small measure be a result of the wisdom and focus of the older women as they provided example and encouragement to the younger women (2:4–5).

Changing patterns of society are such that the passage should be read in today's context not only as a word applicable to the older women but to all those entrusted with the stability of the family. Faithfulness to the marriage vows and service to the children are responsibilities that both the husband and wife need to embrace if the larger peace and security of the family is to be sustained.

Paul hoped that the young church would come to see the doctrine as a bridge to the grace that only Christ's love affords.

Men may love Paul when he instructs the women to be "submissive" (2:5). But in doing so, they ignore the societal context in which Paul wrote. They also overlook Paul's teaching in Galatians 3:28 that in Christ Jesus "there is no longer male and female." Too, they fail to apply Paul's teaching in Ephesians 5:25 that husbands are to "love [their] wives, just as Christ loved the church and gave himself up for her."

The need to interpret Scripture in light of society's changing norms is apparent in Paul's instruction to slaves to remain "submissive" (Titus 2:9). People who attempt to interpret the Bible literally have a tough time with this passage because they have to acknowledge that when it comes to the issue of slaves, they can no longer read God's word literally. Times have changed. Most people no longer accept a biblical teaching that affirms slavery. Paul's point was that integrity and purity of the heart must be the norm by which the Christian is to live.

Conclusion

God's love is the end to which sound doctrine points. Doctrine has its end not in circumcision or other outward appearances of faith; not in the adherence to the letter of the law; but simply in authentic *agape* love. If anything, sound doctrine should remind us that we are broken and in need not of the judgment of the law, but rather the grace of Jesus Christ, which alone can save and satisfy.

> *. . . Sound doctrine should remind us that we are broken and in need not of the judgment of the law, but rather the grace of Jesus Christ, which alone can save and satisfy.*

The way of Christian love is the end to which we are called. In contrast to the passions of the world (2:12) is the gift of grace that allows the freedom to be godly.

Jesus reminded his disciples that the key to finding meaning in life is the willingness to give up one's life for the sake of the gospel (Matthew 10:39). Jesus' point was that one cannot experience true freedom and peace until Christ is the focus. This is Paul's point as well. Sound doctrine is the means by which we focus on the invitation to emulate Christ's love to a world in need not of our theology but rather of Christ's divine heart.

May our prayer be that we will boast of nothing but the Lord. In our boasting of the Lord, each of us has the opportunity to convey the true way of grace that frees us to experience and be Christ's peace in a world that needs his love.

Legalism and Christ

Paul often encountered missionaries who insisted that new converts follow the Jewish law in order to be fully right before God. Specifically, the men had to partake in the Jewish rite of circumcision (see Genesis 17:10–14). Paul's opponents argued that while the new covenant was now available to all, it did not negate the covenant God had made with Abraham.

Such a restrictive view infuriated Paul. He responded to this legalistic view by saying, "For in Christ Jesus neither circumcision nor uncircumcision counts for anything; the only thing that counts is faith working through love" (Galatians 5:10).

Making "Sound Doctrine" Meaningful

- Take time to pray about your attitude and perspective in matters of theology.

- Recognize that the measure of "sound doctrine" must always be the heart of Jesus.

- Emphasize healing and hope, not hindrances and hurt.

- Focus your life in heart and deed on God's grace and mercy.

- Ground a concern for sound doctrine in humility and a willingness to forgive.

Questions

1. When is theology helpful?

2. When is theology destructive?

3. How might "the fruit of the Sprit" of which Paul speaks of in Galatians 5:22–23 be applicable to his emphasis in this lesson on sound doctrine?

4. What is the relationship between theology and the circumstances and experiences of one's life?

5. What are some lessons to be learned, if any, from Paul's encounter with the legalists who insisted on circumcision as a part of the covenant of faith?

NOTES

1. Scripture taken from *The Message.* Copyright © 1993, 1994, 1995, 1996, 2000, 2001, 2002.
2. Some translations use the word "elder," but the Greek word used here is *presbútidas*, which means an older man or woman, and is different from *presbutéros*, which refers to a Jewish religious leader or a leader in the early church (compare with Titus 1:5, for example).

Main Idea

Genuine Christianity means placing priority on eternal life with God rather than focusing on lesser things.

Question to Explore

What does Christianity mean to you?

LESSON TWELVE
Bottom-Line Christianity

Study Aim

To identify practical ways for placing priority on eternal life with God rather than on lesser things

Study and Action Emphases

- Affirm the Bible as our authoritative guide for life and ministry
- Share the gospel with all people
- Develop a growing, vibrant faith

aug 20

Quick Read

Paul detailed in this chapter appropriate Christian conduct in the world guided by the hope and promise of eternal life through God's mercy and grace.

There seemed to be a million things to do to get the children ready for school that morning. I am sure we looked like a family of ants whose nest had been stirred. This was a typical morning, but in the process of getting the day started, the not-so-typical question was asked.

One of the boys wanted to know, "Has God ever spoken to you?"

I thought for a minute about how to respond. Has God ever really spoken to me? After a few seconds of reflection, I responded, "Yes."

But the next set of questions proved even harder to answer. "Really? What did God sound like? What did God say? How can you be sure it was God?"

How does one answer questions like these? How do you explain faith in God, let alone faith in God's presence, without sounding like some crazed soul who hears voices in the dark? I thought about how to respond. How would you? I have to admit I was thinking to myself, *Why did this question have to be asked? It's too early to deal with something this complex.* The moment was not one I would have chosen for such a conversation, but you can't choose the moments when you talk about faith with the kids. I decided to tell the story the children had heard a thousand times before, but in a way that would get at the heart of the question—*Has God ever spoken to you?*

I played on a football team in high school. What else did one do in Georgia for a pastime in the days of my youth? But it wasn't just any football team. We were good. In fact, my senior year, we not only won the high school state championship, but Associated Press ranked the team as the best high school team in the nation! In fact, the year before, we were supposed to have won it all, but we lost a conference game in the closing seconds when the cross-town rivals scored on a *Hail Mary* pass. The loss was bitter. Immediately, I resolved along with my teammates that we would begin even in the midst of that hurt to recommit ourselves to the task of winning. The team, in time, came together. Everybody made it our one goal to win, and winning the state championship became the one and only concern of my life.

"The interesting thing," I said to the children, "was the conversation I had with myself when we finally won the state championship."

Of course, the question that followed was, "What do you mean?"

I explained by saying, "I remember walking off the field thinking, *Just what is it to which you have given your life? In a week, who will remember? In a year, who will care?*" I went on to say to them that the real question I pondered was, *Isn't it about time you start giving your life to something that matters; to something that has eternal consequences?* Then, I said, "I can't explain it, but that one reflective conversation with myself changed my life, and while I can't tell you what God sounded like, I do believe that was the presence of God stirring my soul."

I didn't know it at the time, but the theologian Paul Tillich would much later help me to understand the tension between secondary objectives and a life of service lived for God. Tillich observed that because the holy is ultimately a mystery that no one can fully fathom, the temptation is to give our lives to things that in reality have no redemptive value.[1] In other words, because we can't see and touch God, we find other things that we convince ourselves are really worthy of the Holy. Think of the golden calf the Hebrews created when they got tired of waiting on Moses to report his conversation with God (Exodus 32).

We are not different. Those things—like career, power, wealth, and winning—we convince ourselves are worthy pursuits. We give our lives to their noble end because of the security we believe they will provide, but such endeavors can also control us. Their alluring promise can make us slaves to the kingdoms that we promise to serve. The freedom we thought such goals would provide leaves us feeling empty. Why? Because in the end they carry us no further into the heart of the holy, which is the peace that passes all understanding.

Titus 3:1–9

[1]Remind them to be subject to rulers and authorities, to be obedient, to be ready for every good work,

2to speak evil of no one, to avoid quarreling, to be gentle, and to show every courtesy to everyone. **3**For we ourselves were once foolish, disobedient, led astray, slaves to various passions and pleasures, passing our days in malice and envy, despicable, hating one another. **4**But when the goodness and loving kindness of God our Savior appeared, **5**he saved us, not because of any works of righteousness that we had done, but according to his mercy, through the water of rebirth and renewal by the Holy Spirit. **6**This Spirit he poured out on us richly through Jesus Christ our Savior, **7**so that, having been justified by his grace, we might become heirs according to the hope of eternal life. **8**The saying is sure.

I desire that you insist on these things, so that those who have come to believe in God may be careful to devote themselves to good works; these things are excellent and profitable to everyone. **9**But avoid stupid controversies, genealogies, dissensions, and quarrels about the law, for they are unprofitable and worthless.

The Point of Living Is the Promise of Eternal Life (3:4–7)

Paul detailed in Titus 3 appropriate Christian conduct in the world guided by the end to which the Christian should live, which is the promise of eternal life. Before looking at what Paul instructed Titus to remind his flock about in 3:1–3, look at the reason behind the instructions. The guiding passage of this chapter is the promise that God has saved "through the water of rebirth and renewal by the Holy Spirit . . . poured out on us richly through Jesus Christ our Savior . . . so that, having been justified by his grace, we might become heirs according to the hope of eternal life" (Titus 3:4–7).

Notice the Trinitarian language involved in the promise of salvation ("God our Savior," 3:4; "Holy Spirit," 3:5; "Jesus Christ our Savior," 3:6). Salvation is a result of the initiative of God's mercy. The divine has saved through the Holy Spirit's cleansing, making it possible for the gift of grace to be received in Jesus Christ. The effective agent of cleansing is not the water but the Spirit. The water clearly connotes the centrality of baptism in the early church, but the point of emphasis is the Trinitarian act of God.

Rather than being enslaved to sin, we are to serve and obey God. To do so is to be free to serve in love. . . .

The Greek word translated "rebirth" is a word typically associated with the new world that is to result in the kingdom of God (3:5; see Matthew 19:28, where the word is also used). The word translated "renewal," on the other hand (see Romans 12:2), is associated with the transformation of the individual. (See the article, "'Rebirth' and 'Renewal'" in this lesson.)

These words indicate that salvation thus is redemptive for both the individual and the community. Too often, we who make up the Christian church in the United States think of salvation strictly in terms of the individual. Yet, we need to understand from a biblical context that God is concerned not only about the redemption of the individual. God, too, is concerned about the making of a new world, and there is much need for the contemporary church to begin anew to link the spiritual condition of individuals with the spiritual condition of the church universal through which the new kingdom will be manifest. In short, we are our neighbor's keeper, and we don't get to choose who our neighbor might be.

Christian Conduct and Submissiveness to the State (3:1–2)

In Titus 3, Paul detailed various places in the Christian life where faith is to be guided by this promise of eternal life. As the previous lesson dealt with Christian living in the household of faith, this lesson deals with Christian living

"Has God ever spoken to you?"

in the larger world. At issue is the extent to which faith has real and tangible, even audible, meaning, in a restless sea of chaos and confusion.

Paul called believers "to be subject"—submissive— to rulers and authorities (3:1). Why? The Cretans were known to be an unruly lot (1:10–13). In the previous lesson, the point was made that the purpose of submissiveness in the family was to give witness to the love that Christ embodied. Likewise, in a world not cognizant of the meaning of incarnation, submissiveness was a way to emulate Christ's love and therefore give witness to it.

That Paul also called on Titus to remind the church "to be obedient" (3:1) may suggest that the Roman state had yet to command worship of the emperor. In no way was Paul suggesting that the state and its leaders are beyond question or reproach. As theologian and preacher Helmut Thielicke has observed, for the Christian the state always operates under the guise of "the nevertheless," which means that obedience to the state is always contingent on the state's obedience to the saving history of God most fully revealed in the life and ethics of Jesus Christ.[2]

> *How do you explain faith in God, let alone faith in God's presence, without sounding like some crazed soul who hears voices in the dark?*

Christian Conduct and Obedience to God (3:3)

Obedience is the key to devotion to God and the life of freedom that follows one's service in faith. The notion is a strange one to be sure. How can one be free and yet be enslaved to God?

Paul wrote Titus, "For we ourselves were once foolish, disobedient, led astray, slaves to various passions and pleasures, passing our days in malice and envy, despicable, hating one another" (3:3). Paul had already addressed his concern about the enslavement of sin in his Letter to the Romans. To the church at Rome, Paul observed, "Do you not know that if you present yourselves to anyone as obedient slaves, you are slaves of the one whom you obey, either of sin, which leads to death, or of obedience, which leads to righteousness?" (Romans 6:16). Jesus himself said, "No one can serve two masters" (Matthew 6:24). Rather than being enslaved to sin, we are to serve and obey God. To do so is to be free to serve in love, as we shall see in the next section.

"Good Works," Not "Stupid Controversies" (3:8–9)

"Has God ever spoken to you?" What a question! The reality is, however, that God is always speaking. The larger question is, *Who is listening?* Giving our all to win in the world may have pure intentions. We want to provide for our families. We want them to feel secure. But how in our efforts to win do we reveal our faith to our family and to the larger world? What is the driving motivation of our lives? What are the futile "stupid controversies" (3:9) and endeavors that we pursue? Conversely, what are the "good works" to which God has called us? Paul was well aware that good works don't lead to salvation (see Rom. 3:23–24). Good works are the result of God's mercy that allows us to give ourselves completely to God. To be enslaved to God is to be free to serve in love.

One key to understanding Paul's perspective for our time is found in a related passage in 2 Timothy. There Paul wrote, "Remind them of this, and warn them before God that they are to avoid wrangling over words, which does no good but only ruins those who are listening" (2 Timothy 2:14). Paul added in this lesson's text that the believer is to "avoid stupid controversies, genealogies, dissensions, and quarrels about the law, for they are unprofitable and worthless" (Titus 3:9). Recall the Judaizers of Titus 1 (see comments in lesson 11 under the heading, "The Value of Sound Doctrine"). The Judaizers insisted that believers be circumcised as the sign of their thorough Jewishness prior to being recognized as followers of Christ. Paul's admonition to Titus was to stay clear of such pointless controversy by keeping an eye only on that which is profitable. For Paul, that which is profitable can be experienced only in the regeneration and renewal of the Holy Spirit that leads to salvation in Jesus Christ (3:5–6).

Caught up in our world of getting whatever it is that we want, do we even listen or think about the larger purposes that God wills for our lives?

Similarly, the witness of the church to the world must be to that which alone is spiritually profitable. In a nation so divided about ethical issues and which political party best represents the ethics of kingdom living, perhaps the call to submissiveness for our time has its relevance in helping people within the church and outside it to understand how to engage in conversation once again. We talk past each other. We argue with each other. We no longer relate because we no longer listen. Perhaps one of the greatest revivals of transformation that the contemporary church might offer the nation and the world is the art of submissiveness as modeled by humble servants committed to the conversation of love and acceptance, even as Christ has accepted each of us.

> *. . . That which is profitable can be experienced only in the regeneration and renewal of the Holy Spirit that leads to salvation in Jesus Christ (3:5–6).*

Conclusion

The movie *Cinderella Man* tells the story of Depression-era fighter and folk hero Jim Braddock. He defeated heavyweight champ Max Baer in a fifteen-round slugfest on June 13, 1935. The boxer James J. Braddock fought the fight of a lifetime. His famous opponent, Max Baer, was a grueling champion who was supposed to win and destroy Braddock in the first round of the fight. Braddock had become known as the "Cinderella Man" because he had fought his way against all odds to succeed again. He had been knocked down by physical injury and then the Great Depression.

But Braddock did not quit, even in the face of adversity. The harsh conditions even changed him, giving him a sense of direction about meaning and purpose that he had never realized when life was easier. After several years of struggle, Braddock was given the chance to fight again. Against all odds, he began to succeed. He became a symbol for working people in their struggle to beat the Great Depression and stand again.

When we have been baptized by water and the fire of the Holy Spirit, we know that the hope that springs eternal is life everlasting.

When a reporter asked him about the new sense of resolve in his quest to be the World Champion, Braddock responded by saying, "I now know what I am fighting for." The reporter shot back, "And what's that? What are you fighting for?" Braddock said, "Milk."

Braddock had come to the point where winning and the notoriety it brings were no longer an issue or desire. He was doing what he did not for fame, power, or glory, but because of his love for his children and his wife. No longer did he dream of world titles, but rather focused on the more immediate need to keep his family together, feed them, and pay for the basic utilities of water, heat, and electricity. Granted, Braddock was not perfect. Surely there were selfish motives in his quest, but his experience does elevate for us the question concerning what is important in this life.

"What are you fighting for?" Asked differently, *Has God spoken to you?* Caught up in our world of getting whatever it is that we want, do we even listen or think about the larger purposes that God wills for our lives? Paul knew that the place to which the Christian is called is eternal life with God—not just for the world to come but in the present as well. When we have been baptized by water and the fire of the Holy Spirit, we know that the hope that springs eternal is life everlasting.

"Rebirth" and "Renewal"

Understanding something of the nuances in the Greek language will be helpful in interpreting the implied differences between "rebirth" (Greek, *paliggenesia*) and "renewal" (Greek, *anakainosis*) in Titus 3:5. *Paliggenesia* can be translated as *new birth, reproduction, renewal, recreation,* or *regeneration.* The only other place in the New Testament where this word is found is Matthew 19:28, which refers to the messianic new world that will be instituted for those whose sign of faith is the willingness to sell what they have, give it to the poor, and follow Jesus (Matthew 19:16–22). *Anakainosis* can be translated as *renewal, renovation,* or *complete change for the better.* Its biblical focus is on the individual rather than the community, as seen in Romans 12:2. Paul used this word to indicate that the active imparting of the Holy Spirit is the saving work of God alone.

Questions

1. Can you recall times in your life when God has spoken to you?

2. How do you know it was God who spoke?

3. What does *calling* mean to you? Can one work in the world and be called to minister for Jesus?

4. What is the relationship between Christian works and God's mercy through salvation in Jesus Christ?

NOTES

1. Paul Tillich, *Dynamics of Faith* (New York: Harper & Row Publishers, 1957), 12–16.
2. Helmut Thielicke, *Theological Ethics*, vol. 2, ed. William H. Lazareth (Grand Rapids: William B. Eerdmans Publishing Company, 1979), 322.

Introducing

PHILEMON: *The Gospel Transforming Human Relationships*

The little Book of Philemon is so brief that it is not divided into chapters, but it packs a message far beyond its size. The book centers on Onesimus, a runaway slave who had found Paul and become a Christian (Philemon 10). Onesimus now was providing service to Paul in his "imprisonment for the gospel" (Philem. 13).

Personal in tone, the letter is a masterful exercise in the art of persuasion. Paul wanted Onesimus to be released from slavery in order to continue to be of service to him. In making the "appeal" rather than a "command" (Philem. 8), Paul tugged at every string on Philemon's heart and sense of Christian commitment.[1]

As you study this brief book, consider how Paul's making this request would have affected Onesimus and how granting it would have affected Philemon. When you do, you likely will also be led to consider how the gospel, when genuinely applied, can transcend human barriers and transform human relationships even today. Do you know any human barriers that need to be broken down today? Do you know any relationships that need transforming?

PHILEMON: THE GOSPEL TRANSFORMING
HUMAN RELATIONSHIPS

Lesson 13. The Gospel Transforming Human   Philemon
Relationships

Additional Resources for Studying Philemon[2]

Cain Hope Felder. "The Letter to Philemon." *The New Interpreter's Bible*. Volume XI. Nashville, Tennessee: Abingdon Press, 2000.

Ralph Martin. *Ephesians, Colossians, and Philemon.* Interpretation: A Bible Commentary for Teaching and Preaching. Atlanta: John Knox Press, 1991.

Ray F. Robbins. "Philemon." *The Broadman Bible Commentary.* Volume 11. Nashville, Tennessee: Broadman Press, 1971.

A. T. Robertson. *Word Pictures in the New Testament.* Volume IV. Nashville, Tennessee: Broadman Press, 1931.

NOTES

1. Unless otherwise indicated, all Scripture quotations in this introduction and the lesson on Philemon are from the New Revised Standard Version.
2. Listing a book does not imply full agreement by the writers or BAPTISTWAY PRESS® with all of its comments.

Focal Text
Philemon

Background
Philemon

Main Idea
When Christians live the gospel of Christ, human barriers to fellowship fall and human relationships are transformed.

Question to Explore
How can we allow Christ to draw us closer to fellow Christians who are different from us?

LESSON THIRTEEN
The Gospel Transforming Human Relationships

Study Aim
To decide on actions I will take to draw closer to fellow Christians who are different from me

Study and Action Emphases

- Affirm the Bible as our authoritative guide for life and ministry
- Share the gospel with all people
- Develop a growing, vibrant faith
- Value all people as created in the image of God
- Obey and serve Jesus by meeting physical, spiritual, and emotional needs
- Equip people for servant leadership

Quick Read

Paul's Letter to Philemon on behalf of Onesimus is brief, but it packs an important message—the gospel of Jesus Christ can transform lives and relationships.

If someone were to ask you to identify Paul's most influential or inspirational epistle, how would you respond? You might say Romans, 1 Corinthians, Galatians, or even Philippians. In all probability, however, you would not answer Philemon. This little letter is positioned last among the thirteen letters attributed to Paul due to both its contents and its size. It does not tend to attract the same amount of attention as some of the Apostle's longer letters do. Even so, Paul's Letter to Philemon packs an important message—the gospel of Jesus Christ can transform lives and relationships.

In this lesson we will examine the letter and consider how we might best appropriate its message in our own lives. Before doing so, however, let us first orient ourselves to the story behind the letter and the characters within it.

We do not know precisely why, when, or where, but Onesimus, a slave of Philemon, crossed paths with Paul. Paul was at that time imprisoned. As a result of this encounter with Paul, Onesimus was converted to faith in Christ (Philemon 10). In reading the letter we also learn that some kind of tension likely existed between Philemon and Onesimus (Philem.15, 18–19).

Interpreters of Philemon have traditionally suggested that the conflict between the two resulted from Onesimus running away from his master. More recently, however, some commentators have proposed that Onesimus intentionally sought out Paul as a trusted friend of Philemon's to ask for help in repairing a relational rupture between him and his master. Whatever the case, from Paul's place of captivity, Paul sent Onesimus back to Philemon with a letter (Philem.12). Fortunately, we now have the opportunity to read this carefully crafted letter over Philemon's shoulder.

Philemon

¹Paul, a prisoner of Christ Jesus, and Timothy our brother,

To Philemon our dear friend and co-worker, ²to Apphia our sister, to Archippus our fellow soldier, and to the church in your house:

³Grace to you and peace from God our Father and the Lord Jesus Christ.

⁴When I remember you in my prayers, I always thank my God ⁵because I hear of your love for all the saints and your faith toward the Lord Jesus. ⁶I pray that the sharing of your faith may become effective when you perceive all the good that we may do for Christ. ⁷I have indeed received much joy and encouragement from your love, because the hearts of the saints have been refreshed through you, my brother.

⁸For this reason, though I am bold enough in Christ to command you to do your duty, ⁹yet I would rather appeal to you on the basis of love—and I, Paul, do this as an old man, and now also as a prisoner of Christ Jesus. ¹⁰I am appealing to you for my child, Onesimus,

whose father I have become during my imprisonment. **11**Formerly he was useless to you, but now he is indeed useful both to you and to me. **12**I am sending him, that is, my own heart, back to you. **13**I wanted to keep him with me, so that he might be of service to me in your place during my imprisonment for the gospel; **14**but I preferred to do nothing without your consent, in order that your good deed might be voluntary and not something forced. **15**Perhaps this is the reason he was separated from you for a while, so that you might have him back forever, **16**no longer as a slave but more than a slave, a beloved brother—especially to me but how much more to you, both in the flesh and in the Lord.

17So if you consider me your partner, welcome him as you would welcome me. **18**If he has wronged you in any way, or owes you anything, charge that to my account. **19**I, Paul, am writing this with my own hand: I will repay it. I say nothing about your owing me even your own self. **20**Yes, brother, let me have this benefit from you in the Lord! Refresh my heart in Christ. **21**Confident of your obedience, I am writing to you, knowing that you will do even more than I say.

22One thing more—prepare a guest room for me, for I am hoping through your prayers to be restored to you.

23Epaphras, my fellow prisoner in Christ Jesus, sends greetings to you, **24**and so do Mark, Aristarchus, Demas, and Luke, my fellow workers.

25The grace of the Lord Jesus Christ be with your spirit.

Setting the Stage (1–7)

Paul began his Letter to Philemon in typical Pauline fashion, namely, with a salutation. He commenced his greeting by depicting himself as a prisoner and his co-sender Timothy as "our brother," that is, a believer and perhaps also a co-worker. The principal recipient of the letter was Philemon. Paul described him as both a beloved brother and a fellow laborer in Christ.

Although Paul wrote this letter primarily to Philemon, it was not exclusively to him. Verse 2 indicates as much. In this verse Paul also addressed a certain Apphia and Archippus, who are referred to as "the sister" and "the fellow soldier" respectively (author's translation). They might be related to Philemon (Philemon's wife and son?), but of this we cannot be certain. Like Timothy, Apphia was a believer and probably a Christian laborer. Archippus was a fellow soldier, meaning that he was enlisted in the Lord's service (see also Colossians 4:17).

In addition to those mentioned by name, Paul also addressed his letter to those believers who were a part of the church that met in Philemon's house. The earliest Christian congregations met in people's homes, not in church buildings (note also Romans 16:5, 23; Col. 4:15).

Colossians 4:9 identifies Onesimus as coming from Colossae. So interpreters usually suggest that Philemon lived in Colossae.

Following a succinct greeting (Philem. 3, "Grace ... peace"), Paul conveyed his thanksgiving to God for Philemon (v. 4). Specifically, Paul mentioned the love and faithfulness Philemon displayed toward other believers and toward the Lord Jesus (v. 5). Additionally, Paul expressed his hope that Philemon's faithful partnership in the work of the gospel would continue to contribute to the cause of Christ (v. 6). In concluding his thanksgiving, Paul indicated that Philemon's concrete expressions of love had been a source of joy and comfort to him and a source of spiritual renewal and revitalization for other Christians (v. 7).

> *As a result of this encounter with Paul, Onesimus was converted to faith in Christ (Philemon 10).*

Making a Plea for Onesimus (8–19)

Paul revealed near the outset of this section his reason for writing to Philemon in the first place. By way of transition and prior to making his request, Paul maintained that he possessed adequate boldness or confidence in Christ to command Philemon to do what was fitting. Nonetheless, Paul would rather appeal to him out of love (vv. 8–9a). Furthermore, before announcing his specific plea, Paul depicted himself as a *presbytēs*, a word that scholars have rendered as both *aged man* and *ambassador*. Although the former seems preferable, the latter is possible.

Additionally, Paul reiterated that he was a prisoner of or for Jesus Christ (v. 9b; see again v. 1).

Paul had indicated his preference to appeal lovingly to Philemon instead of boldly ordering him what to do. Now Paul started to set forth his plea for one of whom he initially spoke as his child whom he had fathered while in prison (v. 10). This description depicts the conversion of Onesimus through the witness of Paul. Only after this tender description did Paul at long last specifically mention Onesimus by name (v. 10).

Paul's description of Onesimus as "my child" as opposed to Philemon's slave is significant. It is also important to note in verse 11 Paul's pun on Onesimus's name. The name *Onesimus* means *useful* or *beneficial*. Too, there was in all likelihood at least some reason for Philemon to devalue his slave. So Paul wrote, "Formerly he was useless to you, but now he is useful both to you and to me."

If one were to inquire as to why Onesimus was once "useless" but now "useful," an answer might be forthcoming in yet another play on his name. In the past, Paul stated, Onesimus was *achrēstos* ("useless"), but now, Paul contends, he was *euchrēstos* ("useful"). Interpreters have suggested that in Paul's day the Greek word for Christ (*Christos*) would have been pronounced the same as *chrēstos* ("useful"). If this were in fact the case, then the earliest recipients of Philemon might have inferred that Onesimus's birth into the faith in some sense increased his usefulness both to his master and to his "father" (Philem. 10).

Although the particular reason(s) that Paul appealed to Philemon for Onesimus is (are) now lost on us, verse 12 makes it clear why Paul set forth his plea in the first place. Paul was sending Onesimus back to Philemon. Despite the fact that Onesimus had become especially dear and helpful to Paul in Paul's imprisonment, Paul decided to send him home. One gathers that this was an agonizing decision for Paul. If it had been Paul's prerogative, he would have kept Onesimus to serve alongside him in his imprisonment for the gospel. In so doing, Onesimus would have been, Paul suggested, a sort of surrogate for Philemon (v. 13). Paul was unwilling to keep Onesimus with him without Philemon's willful consent. To have done so would have been inappropriate for a number of reasons, not the least of which was that Onesimus was technically Philemon's property. Paul's stated rationale for sending Onesimus back to Philemon with a letter of intercession, however, was his desire to empower Philemon to exercise his goodness and generosity freely and not under compulsion or pressure (v. 14).

Paul mentioned the love and faithfulness Philemon displayed toward other believers and toward the Lord Jesus (v. 5).

Were Paul to have ended his Letter to Philemon at verse 14, then it would be clear enough what he was asking regarding Onesimus. Verses 13–14 suggest that on Onesimus's return Philemon should turn right around and send him back to Paul. As it happens, this may well be precisely what Paul was requesting. Verses 15–16, however, seem to send another signal. In these verses Paul pondered whether it was part of the divine plan for Onesimus to be separated from Philemon for a season (literally *for an hour*) in order that he might have him back forever, although "no longer as a slave, but much more than a slave, as a beloved brother" (v. 16). Here Paul seemed to envision a temporary, not a protracted, separation of Onesimus from Philemon.

Because they were both believers in Christ, they were now "brothers," not simply slave and master. . . .

Whatever the case, Paul declared that a transformation of seismic spiritual proportions had transpired between Philemon and Onesimus. Because they were both believers in Christ, they were now "brothers," not simply slave and master, for in Christ there is "neither slave nor free" (Galatians 3:28; see 1 Corinthians 7:21–24; 12:13; Col. 3:11; 3:22—4:1).

Onesimus's status as a slave now paled in comparison to his identity as a Christian. Still, his conversion did not alter the grisly reality of his slavery. What is more, even if Philemon did release him from slavery, Onesimus would still be beholden in some ways to Philemon. Neither did Paul call for the eradication of slavery here or elsewhere in his letters. What Paul did do, however, was admonish Philemon to receive his returning slave even as he would Paul himself, that is, as a brother in Christ and a "partner" in the gospel (v. 17). Additionally, Paul requested that he himself be held responsible for any and all repayment in the event Onesimus had wronged Philemon or was otherwise indebted to him (v. 18). As Martin Luther once noted, what Christ has done for us with respect to the Father, Paul did for Onesimus with respect to Philemon; moreover, we are all *Onesimuses* if we believe.

Concluding the Intercessory Letter (19–25)

To this point in the letter an unknown scribe had been writing what Paul had been dictating (see Romans 16:22). Beginning in verse 19, however, and presumably until the end of the letter, Paul did the writing himself. As he took up the pen, he reiterated that he would pay Philemon whatever debt Onesimus owed. But in doing so Paul gently reminded Philemon that he owed him his very self. This statement almost assuredly refers to the fact that Paul had also led Philemon to faith in Christ.

Paul declared that a transformation of seismic spiritual proportions had transpired between Philemon and Onesimus.

Paul turned in verse 20 to ask Philemon to extend to him some benefit in the Lord and to refresh his "heart in Christ." There is more to this verse than meets the eye. Paul's desire for benefit from Philemon is seemingly another play on Onesimus's name. Consider for yourself the similarity between Onesimus (*Onēsimos* in Greek) and the verb Paul employed that we in turn render "I wish or desire benefit" (author's translation; Greek, *oninēmi*). If this remark is best taken as an intentional allusion to Onesimus, then the argument that Paul's desire is for Philemon to receive Onesimus warmly and then return him promptly to Paul in prison is strengthened.

When Paul asked Philemon to refresh his heart in Christ, he was in effect asking Philemon to do for him that which he had done already for other believers (v. 7). Moreover, one should note that Paul employed the same Greek word in verse 20 (*splagchnon*, translated "heart") that he did in verse 12 when he indicated that by sending Onesimus back to Philemon he was sending his "heart" (*splagchnon*). If Onesimus was Paul's "heart," then by asking Philemon to refresh his "heart" in Christ was Paul also asking for similar refreshment for Onesimus?

> *. . . Paul gently reminded Philemon that he owed him his very self.*

Moving to verse 21, Paul indicated that he had written Philemon due to a sense of confidence in Philemon's obedience. Indeed, Paul remarked that he knew Philemon would do above and beyond that which Paul had requested.

Verse 21 raises at least two questions: To whom was Philemon meant to be obedient, and what was it that Paul had actually asked Philemon to do? Although Paul indicated he had no desire to command Philemon what to do (v. 8), he did anticipate that Philemon would comply with his request regarding Onesimus, whatever that might be (see especially v. 17). In so doing Philemon would not only honor Paul's request but would also be obeying God. Paul hoped that Philemon's response to his plea would be so positive that it would go beyond what he had written and would honor the intentions that gave rise to his writing in the first place.

As Paul concluded his correspondence to Philemon, he asked him to ready a guest room for him. Paul was hopeful that he would be able to visit Philemon as God enabled his release from captivity in answer to the prayers of Philemon and the church that gathered in his home (v. 22). This request reinforced the partnership that Paul and Philemon shared. It also served as a subtle reminder that Philemon might well have to give an account to Paul in person regarding his dealing with Onesimus.

> Paul hoped that Philemon's response to his plea would be so positive that it would go beyond what he had written. . . .

Finally, in verses 23–24 Paul sent Philemon greetings from his fellow prisoner (Epaphras) and his fellow workers (Mark, Aristarchus, Demas, and Luke). The close correlation between the people mentioned in Philemon and those mentioned in Colossians 4:7–17 has led many commentators to suggest that these letters were written around the same time and from the same place. The options offered are Ephesus (about A.D. 53–56), Caesarea (about A.D. 57–59), and Rome (about A.D. 60–62).

An extension of grace to Philemon and those with whom he lived and worshiped concludes this fascinating letter (v. 25).

Slavery

Although the Letter to Philemon is not a treatise on slavery, Onesimus is described as a slave (Philem.16). The very mention of slavery evokes in most American minds the practice of many Southerners in the eighteenth and nineteenth century.

This fact notwithstanding, interpreters of Paul's Letter to Philemon would do well to recognize that there is not a one-for-one correlation between slavery in the Greco-Roman world and its counterpart in the American South. To be sure, in both incarnations of this evil, people were perceived and treated as property. They typically lived and died under brutal conditions. Nonetheless, in Paul's day, slavery was not based on race. Furthermore, in New Testament times slaves were integrated into society, could achieve some professional and legal standing, and were often released from enslavement (the technical term is manumission). That Paul and his Christian contemporaries could not envision the abolition of slavery and did not tend to question the institution is not as surprising or as disappointing as the perpetuation and support of this blight by many church leaders and members until relatively recent times.

Onesimus

Around the turn of the first century A.D., Ignatius was bishop of the church in Syrian Antioch, and he wrote a letter to Ephesian Christians.[1] Near the outset of this letter, Ignatius referred to one Onesimus as the bishop of the Ephesian church. Ignatius described him as a person of "inexpressible love." Scholars have suggested that this is the same Onesimus of whom Paul spoke in Philemon. Should this later literary reference influence the way we interpret Paul's Letter to Philemon? How?

Questions

1. What are some of the Christian convictions that are detectable in Philemon?

2. If you had written Philemon, what, if anything, would you have done differently?

3. Did Paul see slavery as incompatible with Christianity? Why or why not?

4. How would you have responded to Paul's letter if you were Philemon?

5. Why might Paul's Letter to Philemon have been included in the New Testament?

NOTES

1. Ignatius, *To the Ephesians* 1.3.

PSALMS AND PROVERBS:
Songs and Sayings of Faith

THE BOOK OF PSALMS: SONGS OF FAITH

Lesson 1.	The Way to True Happiness	Psalm 1
Lesson 2.	Pleading for God's Help	Psalms 3:1–8; 13:1–6; 22:1–5, 22–24
Lesson 3.	Trusting in a Caring God	Psalms 23:1–6; 27:1–6
Lesson 4.	Thirsting for God	Psalms 42—43
Lesson 5.	Almost Doubting	Psalm 73
Lesson 6.	The Joy of Worshiping God Together	Psalm 84
Lesson 7.	To Live a Life That Matters	Psalm 90
Lesson 8.	Praise for God's Goodness	Psalms 100; 103
Lesson 9.	Give Thanks for God's Blessings	Psalm 116

THE BOOK OF PROVERBS: SAYINGS OF FAITH

Lesson 10.	The Beginning of Wisdom	Proverbs 1:7; 3:1–20
Lesson 11.	Wisdom for Right Living	Proverbs 11:1–11, 17–21, 23–25, 28
Lesson 12.	Wisdom for Every Area of Life	Proverbs 22:17–25; 23:10–11, 19–28; 24:10–12, 15–20
Lesson 13.	Wisdom in Human Relationships	Proverbs 25:11–23; 26:18–28

229

Additional Resources for Studying Psalms and Proverbs[1]

W. H. Bellinger, Jr. *Psalms: Reading and Studying the Book of Praises*. Peabody, Massachusetts: Hendrickson Publishers, 1990.

W. H. Bellinger, Jr. *The Testimony of Poets and Sages: The Psalms and Wisdom Literature*. Macon, Georgia: Smyth and Helwys Publishing, Inc., 1997.

Nancy L. deClaissé-Walford. *Introduction to the Psalms: A Song from Ancient Israel*. St. Louis, Missouri: Chalice Press, 2004.

John I. Durham, "Psalms," *The Broadman Bible Commentary*. Volume 4. Nashville, Tennessee: Broadman Press, 1971.

J. Clinton McCann, Jr. "Psalms." *The New Interpreter's Bible*. Volume 4. Nashville: Abingdon Press, 1996.

James Luther Mays. *Psalms*. Interpretation: A Bible Commentary for Teaching and Preaching. Louisville, Kentucky: John Knox Press, 1994.

Marvin E. Tate. "Proverbs." *The Broadman Bible Commentary*. Volume 5. Nashville, Tennessee: Broadman Press, 1971.

Marvin E. Tate. *Psalms 51—100*. Word Biblical Commentary. Waco, Texas: Word, 1990.

Raymond C. Van Leeuwen. "Proverbs." *The New Interpreter's Bible*. Volume 5. Nashville: Abingdon Press, 1997.

NOTES

1. Listing a book does not imply full agreement by the writers or BAPTISTWAY PRESS® with all of its comments.

How to Order More Bible Study Materials

It's easy! Just fill in the following information. For additional Bible study materials, see www.baptistwaypress.org or get a complete order form of available materials by calling 1–866–249–1799 or e-mailing baptistway@bgct.org.

Title of item	Price	Quantity	Cost
This Issue:			
1, 2 Timothy, Titus, Philemon—Study Guide	$2.75	_____	_____
1, 2 Timothy, Titus, Philemon—Large Print Study Guide	$2.85	_____	_____
1, 2 Timothy, Titus, Philemon—Teaching Guide	$3.25	_____	_____
Additional Issues Available:			
Genesis 12–50: Family Matters—Study Guide	$1.95	_____	_____
Genesis 12–50: Family Matters—Large Print Study Guide	$1.95	_____	_____
Genesis 12–50: Family Matters—Teaching Guide	$2.45	_____	_____
Exodus: Freed to Follow God—Study Guide	$2.35	_____	_____
Exodus: Freed to Follow God—Large Print Study Guide	$2.35	_____	_____
Exodus: Freed to Follow God—Teaching Guide	$2.95	_____	_____
Leviticus, Numbers, Deuteronomy—Study Guide	$2.35	_____	_____
Leviticus, Numbers, Deuteronomy—Large Print Study Guide	$2.35	_____	_____
Leviticus, Numbers, Deuteronomy—Teaching Guide	$2.95	_____	_____
Joshua and Judges—Study Guide	$2.35	_____	_____
Joshua and Judges—Large Print Study Guide	$2.35	_____	_____
Joshua and Judges—Teaching Guide	$2.95	_____	_____
1 and 2 Samuel—Study Guide	$2.35	_____	_____
1 and 2 Samuel—Large Print Study Guide	$2.35	_____	_____
1 and 2 Samuel—Teaching Guide	$2.95	_____	_____
Matthew: Jesus' Teachings—Study Guide	$2.35	_____	_____
Matthew: Jesus' Teachings—Large Print Study Guide	$2.35	_____	_____
Matthew: Jesus' Teachings—Teaching Guide	$2.95	_____	_____
Jesus in the Gospel of Mark—Study Guide	$1.95	_____	_____
Jesus in the Gospel of Mark—Large Print Study Guide	$1.95	_____	_____
Jesus in the Gospel of Mark—Teaching Guide	$2.45	_____	_____
Luke: Journeying to the Cross—Study Guide	$2.35	_____	_____
Luke: Journeying to the Cross—Large Print Study Guide	$2.35	_____	_____
Luke: Journeying to the Cross—Teaching Guide	$2.95	_____	_____
1 Corinthians—Study Guide	$1.95	_____	_____
1 Corinthians—Teaching Guide	$2.45	_____	_____
2 Corinthians: Taking Ministry Personally—Study Guide	$2.35	_____	_____
2 Corinthians: Taking Ministry Personally—Large Print Study Guide	$2.35	_____	_____
2 Corinthians: Taking Ministry Personally—Teaching Guide	$2.95	_____	_____
Hebrews and James—Study Guide	$1.95	_____	_____
Hebrews and James—Teaching Guide	$2.45	_____	_____
Letters of John and Peter—Study Guide	$1.95	_____	_____
Letters of John and Peter—Teaching Guide	$2.45	_____	_____
Revelation—Study Guide	$2.35	_____	_____
Revelation—Large Print Study Guide	$2.35	_____	_____
Revelation—Teaching Guide	$2.95	_____	_____
Coming for use beginning September 2006			
Psalms and Proverbs: Songs and Sayings of Faith—Study Guide	$2.75	_____	_____
Psalms and Proverbs: Songs and Sayings of Faith—Large Print Study Guide	$2.85	_____	_____
Psalms and Proverbs: Songs and Sayings of Faith—Teaching Guide	$3.25	_____	_____

Baptist Doctrine and Heritage

The Bible—You Can Believe It	$4.95	_____	_____
The Bible—You Can Believe It—Teaching Guide	$1.95	_____	_____

Beliefs Important to Baptists

Beliefs Important to Baptists—Study Guide *(one-volume edition; includes all lessons)*	$2.35	_____	_____
Beliefs Important to Baptists—Teaching Guide *(one-volume edition; includes all lessons)*	$1.95	_____	_____
Who in the World Are Baptists, Anyway? (one lesson)	$ .45	_____	_____
Who in the World Are Baptists, Anyway?—Teacher's Edition	$ .55	_____	_____
Beliefs Important to Baptists: I (four lessons)	$1.35	_____	_____
Beliefs Important to Baptists: I—Teacher's Edition	$1.75	_____	_____
Beliefs Important to Baptists: II (four lessons)	$1.35	_____	_____
Beliefs Important to Baptists: II—Teacher's Edition	$1.75	_____	_____
Beliefs Important to Baptists: III (four lessons)	$1.35	_____	_____
Beliefs Important to Baptists: III—Teacher's Edition	$1.75	_____	_____

For Children

Let's Explore Baptist Beliefs	$ 3.95	_____	_____
Let's Explore Baptist Beliefs—Leader's Guide	$ 2.95	_____	_____

Subtotal	_____
Standard Shipping*	
Basic Charge	$6.00
Plus 12% of Subtotal	_____
TOTAL	_____

*Please allow three weeks for standard delivery. For express shipping service:
Call 1–866–249–1799 for information on additional charges.

YOUR NAME   PHONE

YOUR CHURCH   DATE ORDERED

MAILING ADDRESS

CITY   STATE   ZIP CODE

MAIL this form with your check for the total amount to
BAPTISTWAY PRESS, Baptist General Convention of Texas,
333 North Washington, Dallas, TX 75246-1798
(Make checks to "Baptist Executive Board.")

OR, **FAX** your order anytime to: 214-828-5187, and we will bill you.

OR, **CALL** your order toll-free: 1-866-249-1799 (8:30 a.m.-5:00 p.m., M-F),
and we will bill you.

OR, **E-MAIL** your order to our internet e-mail address: baptistway@bgct.org,
and we will bill you.

OR, **ORDER ONLINE** at www.baptistwaypress.org.

We look forward to receiving your order! Thank you!